*As Einstein is often quoted as saying:
No problem can be solved from the same
consciousness that created it. We must learn
to see the world anew.*

—Margaret J. Wheatley

Contents

Preface   vii

Introduction   ix

PART 1
Setting the Stage

1   The New Challenge   3

2   The Role of Mental Models in Professional Development   13

3   How the Brain/Mind Learns   25

4   The Mindshifts Process Groups   41

5   Additional Guidance on the Nature of Process   53

PART 2
Principles of Brain/Mind Learning

6   Principle 1: The Brain Is a Living System   63

7   Principle 2: The Brain/Mind Is Social   79

8   Principle 3: The Search for Meaning Is Innate   91

9   Principle 4: The Search for Meaning Occurs through Patterning   103

10   Principle 5: Emotions Are Critical to Patterning   115

11   Principle 6: Every Brain Simultaneously Perceives and Creates Parts and Wholes   127

12   Principle 7: Learning Involves Both Focused Attention and Peripheral Perception   141

13   Principle 8: Learning Always Involves Conscious and Unconscious Processes   155

14   Principle 9: We Have at Least Two Ways of Organizing
      Memory   167

15   Principle 10: Learning Is Developmental   183

16   Principle 11: Complex Learning Is Enhanced by
      Challenge and Inhibited by Threat Associated with
      a Sense of Helplessness or Fatigue   195

17   Principle 12: Every Brain Is Uniquely Organized   209

PART 3
Making It Happen

18   Reconceptualizing What We Want Students to Learn   221

19   Reconceptualizing Teaching: A Theory of Practice   239

20   Ongoing Professional Development and the Renewal
      of Process   253

Bibliography   263

Index   265

Preface

We must come to a new understanding of learning and teaching so that we can get beyond educating children merely to work in the industries of the twentieth century. It is not just a matter of finding new things to do. It is a matter of profoundly reconceptualizing what we are trying to accomplish.

This process book is written for educators who are interested in meaningful learning. It is not just a recipe book with techniques to boost memorization, though memory in fact does increase dramatically when learning is meaningful. Nor is it a how-to book with techniques that work wonders for educators who do not understand how learning works.

MindShifts is designed to increase your awareness of how the brain learns and to provide you with tools and procedures that enable you to design your own techniques and effective learning environments. It is based on the assumption that, for adults and children alike, meaningful learning is developmental and leads to genuine personal change, and that school restructuring is also developmental and leads to genuine systemic change.

Because all effective learning involves some uncertainty and confusion, what we have written is unlikely to make complete sense after the first reading. You should not expect or seek mastery of any section before you explore another section. Each section is designed to throw light on every other section. Therefore, you can proceed through this process book systematically or dip into sections in any order you prefer. You may even find yourself reworking some sections several times.

All students and all teachers have immeasurable untapped reserves of competence and creativity. As you better appreciate how our brain learns, how it creates and processes information, you will begin to access more of those hidden reserves, as will your students. Then you can better meet the challenge and experience the fulfillment to which we as educators are entitled.

That which is boundless in you
abides in the mansion of the sky,
whose door is the morning mist,
and whose windows are the songs and the silences of the night.

—Kahlil Gibran, *The Prophet*

Introduction

Story Line

This book was designed to assist you in establishing a flexible and powerful foundation for your learning community. You will begin to appreciate the underlying and often invisible patterns around which education forms. And you will set in motion the new patterns that must guide you on the journey upon which you are embarking.

We begin part 1 by suggesting that *educators* have to find a way to solve many problems simultaneously, and we spell out the basic assumptions that have guided us in writing this book. We next introduce a distinction between a theory and a mental model. We also explain the importance of dealing with individual change and systemic change simultaneously. We introduce a way of thinking about learning and teaching. We conclude by setting up unique study groups that we call "Mindshifts process groups."

Part 2 is an in-depth exploration of twelve brain/mind principles. We have included group activities and questions to ask about teaching and learning that challenge taken-for-granted beliefs.

In part 3, we spell out the overall theory upon which brain-based instruction is founded. We provide a larger framework for connecting and integrating the scores of strategies and materials that are now available.

Hints and Ideas for Using This Book

Following are some recommendations to help you gain the maximum return on your time and effort. You will find that the recommendations help you implement and experience directly many of the ideas that we discuss in more depth later.

Explore Our Other Works to Support Your Work

Although *MindShifts* is self-contained, it works in tandem with our other books. *Making Connections: Teaching and the Human Brain* (Caine and Caine 1994) is the book in which we first introduced our theory of brain-based learning. It contains the initial research for our ideas. *Education on the Edge of Possibility* (Caine and Caine 1997a) summarizes and updates the theory. It shows why systems resist change and the ways we need to change our thinking about systems. And it describes in depth the experiences that the three of us had when we took the theory into schools for more than five years. *Unleashing the Power of Perceptual Change* (Caine and Caine 1997d) takes you in depth into the personal qualities educators need to become really sophisticated in their profession. It also describes the developmental path and road map that we believe can help educators on the way. And finally, *The Re-Enchantment of Learning* (Crowell, Caine, and Caine 1997) evokes the spirit of those who have ventured deeply into the realms of personal growth.

You may also find our two videos helpful (Caine and Caine 1997c; Caine, Caine, and Crowell 1997). The first, *Teaching and the Human Brain,* is an overview of significant elements in *Making Connections.* The other, *MindShifts,* demonstrates the process groups described in this book. Finally, our *MindShifts* posters illustrate the principles of connectedness and can be used in a variety of ways.

Take Your Time

Ongoing consistency of effort is much more valuable than one brief, intensive examination of the contents. There are rhythms to learning, in part because meaningful learning engages the entire body, brain, and mind. As you sense those rhythms yourself, you will become better equipped to support them in your students.

Keep a Journal

You will have invaluable insights of your own as you deal with our materials. Such insights may be lost if you do not record them. In fact, keeping a journal actually helps you reflect and have the insights you need. It is one aspect of the active processing of experience that we deal with in depth in other places in this book. We have left spaces throughout for you to record your thoughts, notes, drawings, doodles, and webs, but keeping a journal will increase the benefit you derive from using this book.

Have a Project or Relevant, Personal Application in Mind

Your project or application could be anything from the way you teach a specific subject to the way you approach a new hobby to the way you deal with a social concern over which you wish to have some influence. This project will significantly enhance your own learning.

Use and Experiment with New Techniques and Strategies Frequently

Do *not* decide in advance how the techniques and strategies are going to work or what the effects will be. An immense repertoire of strategies, techniques, and processes are available for you to sample and try in your work. They are not our focus in this book because our goal is more than skill development or "getting it right." The techniques that we describe are designed to generate experiences that provide an overall and deeper sense of how people make meaning and acquire dynamical knowledge or real understanding (see chapter 18). Later, we encourage you to examine, test, and implement techniques from other sources that are congruent with what you have learned about learning and teaching, and to develop further your own mental models. Mental models are the deeply ingrained assumptions and generalizations that influence how you understand the world and how you take action. In other words, try some of your new ideas and see what happens. Learn from your experience.

Cultivate and Welcome Active Uncertainty as a State of Mind

Genuine learning involves genuinely changing our minds. Although we need to relate what we study to what we know, we cannot afford to reduce what we study to what we currently believe and understand. Before our new assumptions can take form, other, well-entrenched beliefs must go. The in-between state, which may involve a sense of confusion and incompleteness, is absolutely vital for our students, and therefore we must accept and understand it in ourselves.

Set up a Process Group to Work through the Ideas and Activities

We have developed a set of guidelines for groups to follow, and we spell them out in depth in chapter 5. However, there are many ways to set up groups within a school and beyond the boundaries of a school. The most important requirement of these groups is that the members reflect in an honest and orderly way upon their individual, personal experiences. They are not problem-solving groups, they do not have a prescribed administrative agenda, and they are not to be controlled by outsiders telling the members what to do.

As the concepts and procedures in this book become part of your dynamical natural knowledge, literally second nature to you, you will change and how you view teaching will change. Such changes may include your sense of time, your definition of learning, your assessment of outcomes, and your view of the school. Begin slowly and gently to build success in your own way and in your own world before you seek to change other teachers, parents, or administrators. We all need to go through the process itself.

Encourage rather than criticize;
Demonstrate rather than tell.

PART 1

Setting the Stage

Once upon a time, on a planet much like ours, there were lots of people who had to make long and hazardous journeys to get from where they were to where they were going. An elite group of tour guides was responsible for leading them. The journeys were often a thousand miles and more, over mountains, across deserts, through swamps. Hostile bands had to be avoided or defeated without anyone's being injured. The guides had to provide food, water, and shelter. Yet more and more people wanted to travel, and they all demanded to arrive in good condition and on time.

The tour guides were fed up. They were overworked, underpaid, highly stressed, and . . . rather annoyed.

During one of their rare breaks, when conditions were even worse than usual, and during a moment of even more uncommon silence, one of their number was heard to say, "I had a strange dream last night. I dreamed that we crossed the mountains and the deserts faster than a speeding bullet, and we had so much free time left that we got to go to planet Earth for a holiday."

So frustrated were her colleagues that they did not dismiss the dream out of hand. Instead there was a question: "How did you do it?"

Silence, then an answer. "We could fly."

Learn to unclutter your mind.
Learn to simplify your work.

—John Heider, *The Tao of Leadership*

1

The New Challenge

As educators we cannot deal in the old way with the mountains and deserts and hostile forces anymore. There are just too many. We have no alternative. We have to learn how to fly, meaning we have to deal with education differently from the ways in which we have dealt with it in the past.

The biggest problem facing educators is that there are too many problems. For example, we have to prepare students to pass tests devised by others, on content selected by others, and both tests and content are constantly changing. For many, classes are full of people from a variety of cultural backgrounds, who often speak languages that we do not know. Students come from backgrounds that may be deprived or enriched, secure or threatening, healthy or drug afflicted. We work with more people than we can manage, with inadequate resources and in content areas that often are not our fields of expertise. And all these problems occur within an administrative system that often seems to be indifferent to the needs of the people in it.

Add to these challenges all the innovations, strategies, and practices that are currently being advocated.

For the first time in history . . . the physical survival of the human race depends on a radical change of the human heart. This is a call to service that will take great courage—to leave what we have and move out, not without fear, but without succumbing to that fear. It is a call to redefine what is possible, to see a vision of a new world and to be willing to undertake, step by step, what is necessary in concrete terms to achieve that vision.

—Joseph Jaworski
Synchronicity

To which of the following issues are you being exposed?

- ❏ authentic assessment
- ❏ whole language
- ❏ thematic instruction
- ❏ integrated curriculum
- ❏ block scheduling
- ❏ multiage grouping
- ❏ constructivism
- ❏ multiculturalism
- ❏ accountability
- ❏ peer coaching
- ❏ changing state and district mandates

- ❏ authentic experience
- ❏ reading recovery
- ❏ multimedia and computers
- ❏ cooperative learning
- ❏ site-based management
- ❏ action research
- ❏ full inclusion
- ❏ multiple intelligences
- ❏ changes in class size
- ❏ phonics-based programs
- ❏ standards and standardized tests

List other issues that are arising or strategies and processes that are being introduced in some way into your professional environment.

To what extent does your situation look and feel hopeless?

The World Is Changing

The most important point is that during times of great change there is a great deal of turbulence and uncertainty, with many conflicting undercurrents. In the following discussion, we outline some of the conflicting undercurrents in education.

Back to Basics

Some people want to go back to the way things were when they were in school, a move that is often called "back to basics." Such a suggestion often happens when people become fearful. It also happens when new approaches are forced into old models. One example of a back-to-basics approach is the move from whole language to phonics or a skills-based approach to teaching reading. In teaching whole language, many teachers thought that if they just read more stories to children, students would simply "pick up" phonics and other specific critical skills. The result, in many cases, was that students failed to learn those basic skills. But the trouble with a wholesale retreat to solely phonics may mean that good elements of whole language get lost along the way, so those who were providing very sophisticated and high quality language and reading instruction to children are penalized, and their students lose out, as well.

With what aspects of the back-to-basics movement are you currently dealing?

A Threatened System

At the same time some are shouting for a back-to-basics move, the larger education system itself seems threatened, on the verge of falling apart and rearranging itself. Following is a list of some current system changes that are in the wind:

- increased home schooling
- more charter schools
- vouchers
- distance education (that is, satellite-fed courses of instruction and teleconferencing)
- business-run schools
- site-based management
- technology partnerships

With which of these are you dealing? To what extent is your school system being rearranged?

It is very difficult to imagine what things are going to look like twenty years from now, so we are faced with parallel challenges:

1. We need to improve the system as it is.

2. We need to prepare for a future that we cannot fully predict.

Taking Charge of Change

Our challenge as educators is to realize that all our problems are connected to one another and they cause one another. We will turn education around, in our classrooms and in our communities, when we adequately grasp the nature of that connectedness. The point is that the way we have been addressing the situation has become self-defeating. We simply cannot succeed by doing things the way they have always been done, which brings the three of us back to our initial point. We have too many problems, and it is not possible to solve them all—one at a time. Yet we still have to find a place to begin.

Our Approach

Every process and procedure is grounded in a set of assumptions about how things work. As authors, we are no exception. We feel that we should spell out our basic assumptions immediately. We invite you to set the stage for your own development by examining our assumptions and, over time, comparing them with your own.

1. **The way in which we educate and teach depends upon our mental models of how people learn.** Peter Senge (1990) notes, "Mental models are deeply ingrained assumptions, generalizations, or even pictures or images that influence how we understand the world and how we take action. Very often, we are not consciously aware of our mental models or the effects they have on our behavior" (8). Senge notes further that there is often a difference between our "espoused theories" (what we say) and our "theories in use"—our mental models. According to Chris Argyris, we do not always act congruently with what we say, but we do act congruently with what we believe (Senge 1990, 175). It is what we actually believe—our mental models—that drives every decision we make and every strategy we select. The primary key to improving students' learning, therefore, is for everyone involved in their education to have a powerful and accurate mental model of how people learn.

2. **Mental models should be based on the best, up-to-date research about how the brain/mind actually learns.** Learning is as natural as breathing. And just as our lungs and respiratory systems have been designed for their functions, so the brain is designed for learning. Fortunately, researchers now know a lot about how the brain does its job. Renate and Geoffrey Caine (1994) translated research into a set of principles and a theory of great practical value for educators. One of our objectives is for educators to understand and internalize, as a mental model that guides them, a sound theory of brain-based learning and teaching.

3. **One of the best ways to enhance or acquire a new mental model is to examine our own experience, and to challenge our assumptions and current beliefs about learning and teaching.** The way in which people become experts always involves examination of their own experience. This principle emerges out of brain research. In fact, it is quite extraordinary that some of the processes we have all used and have become competent in—as we mastered a hobby, for instance—often get left at the door to the classroom. Our own practices are the raw material out of which further expertise emerges. Unfortunately, educators and support staff usually do not have time to reflect upon what they have done and what they have learned. Most reflection is limited to thinking about what has to be done next. Hence we must establish a process, supported by the educational system, that generates and sustains reflection on what and how we have learned.

4. **For a school to change successfully, the adults working in it need to share a core of common beliefs that are reflected in a powerful and accurate mental model of learning so that decisions and interactions are mutually reinforcing.** Perhaps the most important idea is

that change and growth must occur in individual and collective ways. On the one hand, we are all individuals, with beliefs, values, experiences, preferences, and personal styles. On the other hand, we are all members of small and large groups that we influence and that influence what we do. Each of us is called to make countless decisions that have an impact on the school as a whole. We cannot possibly collaborate on everything. It is the totality of our taken-for-granted agreements and underlying beliefs and purposes that will help or hinder systemic change. When all staff members in a school base individual decisions on common underlying ideas, in almost every case the system as a whole is in their minds as well, and the system as a whole will be improved.

5. **The basis for effective long-term change is the creation of a healthy and supportive learning school community, which will make it possible for a new mental model to be implemented.** One principle that emerges from neuroscientific research is that complex learning is inhibited by threat and enhanced by challenge. This principle does not mean that we should never feel anxious, but it does mean that when we feel helpless or fatigued, it is more difficult to learn. The principle applies just as much to us as to our students. Our conclusion is that the first task is to create supportive and healthy learning communities. As Joyce, Wolf, and Calhoun (1993) say, "All personnel become students of school improvement. An integrated culture of professionals is developed." A self-renewing school is a place where all participants are learning, where learning itself is valued, where there is a sense of camaraderie and cooperation, where there is adherence to at least some common values and procedures, and where there is an underlying sense of orderliness and commitment to a common purpose.

6. **There is, and should continue to be, a major shift in the direction of education generally, away from a delivery model of facts and information to a model based on meaningful learning acquired through guided experience.** For the last four hundred years, the dominant mode of thinking in our culture has been mechanistic. The school system developed out of that thinking. People viewed schools as something akin to social machines, which led to a mechanistic approach to instruction and administration that reached its apex in the industrial age. We and others call it the *industrial model* of education. Its core was the delivery of prescribed facts to be memorized and the presentation of basic skills to be mastered. It has become apparent in at least the last twenty years that meaningful learning and high standards depend on embedding the curriculum in practical, complex experiences guided by the teacher but driven by the student. We describe this emerging model as being based on guided experience. The shift toward this model of guided experiences is absolutely indispensable for education to be effective in the twenty-first century.

As you work on your new mental model together you will learn from one another, develop your own points of view, and develop a common perspective—a shared mental model based upon brain research—about teaching, learning, and support. The result will be an emergent atmosphere of mutual respect and support for individual growth and school change.

Until one is committed, there is hesitancy, the chance to draw back, always ineffectiveness, concerning all acts of initiative (and creation). There is one elementary truth the ignorance of which kills countless ideas and splendid plans: that the moment one definitely commits oneself, then Providence moves too. All sorts of things occur to help one that would never otherwise have occurred. A whole stream of events issues from the decisions, raising in one's favor all manner of unforeseen incidents and meetings and material assistance which no man could have dreamed would have come his way. Whatever you can do or dream you can, begin it. Boldness has genius, power, and magic in it. Begin it now.

—Johann Wolfgang von Goethe

2

The Role of Mental Models in Professional Development

Mental models are deeply ingrained assumptions, generalizations, or even pictures or images that influence how we understand the world and how we take actions. Very often, we are not consciously aware of our mental models or the effects they have on our behavior.

—Peter Senge
The Fifth Discipline

Storing information and mastering skills are *not* the most important learning anyone does. Underneath all that learning is something so pervasive that we tend not even to know it is there. At the heart of each person is a set of mental models about how the world works and what life is about. And *all* of our learning, without any exception, goes toward creating, confirming, or testing those models. As Senge indicates, the decisions that we make, the way that we act and react, what we do and what we think are all driven by our mental models.

There is an immediate and practical consequence of trying to solve major, long-term problems, or for embarking upon a process of professional and personal development. The place to begin is not with the problems but with ourselves. More specifically, we have to test our ways of perceiving and thinking about a situation, and if necessary, we have to develop an accurate and powerful new way to be adequately equipped to deal with the situation. This process of examination can lead to practical solutions and applications that did not seem possible before.

Unpacking Fundamental Concepts

One way to begin to examine our theories and actions is to identify some of the central concepts that guide education and unpack them to see what deeper meanings they have for us. In fact, one indicator of change and growth is our deepening appreciation of the meaning and implication of those fundamental concepts. As "learning," "teaching," and "schooling" are among the central ideas that need to be reconceptualized, we will begin with them. This reflective examination allows us to think "outside the box" and imagine something other than "business as usual."

We ask questions that lead you to think about what some of the concepts mean. Whether or not you have thought about them recently, you need to arrive at realistic, personal definitions of them. One useful technique to begin with is brainstorming, then reflecting in writing on what you discover through your brainstorming.

Step 1: Write the basic idea in the center of a page or use the space on these two pages. Then allow as many associations to come to mind as come.

Step 2: Write down your thoughts anywhere on the page.

Step 3: After you have brainstormed every idea you can, find a basic general pattern or idea that explains your central understanding of the concept.

Step 4: Write half a page to a page about what you think the concept really means. You might note the date, as well.

■ **What does learning mean to you?**

- What is teaching?

- Where is school?

- What is the core curriculum?

- Who are a child's most influential teachers?

- What other key concepts or constructs would you like to explore?

As you work through this book, you may want to revisit your responses from time to time and reconsider them in terms of your current appreciation of how we learn.

Imagine walking into a classroom in which the teacher is telling the students the meaning of something they have just read. Imagine walking into another classroom where students are discussing among themselves what a reading means to them and perhaps to others. What underlying beliefs exhibited in each example drive each teacher's approach?

Whenever we do anything, be it asking questions, answering questions, giving advice, or designing a lesson, a personal theory—that is, a mental model—drives us. For example, a mental model might be that children are blank slates waiting to absorb new knowledge the teacher provides. A teacher who has this mental model will think and behave differently from one who has a mental model that children are active meaning makers born to make sense of their world and participate in their own learning. Imagine some consequences derived from these two mental models:

Possible Thoughts of a Teacher Who Believes that Children Are Blank Slates

- I must present the material correctly.
- I can tell when my students have learned because they know the right answers.
- The more information the child can absorb, the better teacher I am.

Possible Thoughts of a Teacher Who Believes that Students Are Active Meaning Makers

- I have to create learning experiences that allow children with various styles and abilities to benefit.
- As much as possible, I need to challenge children to ask their own questions and research possible answers.
- I can tell that my students have learned when they can actively demonstrate in some way what they know to others. They can describe, perform, or exhibit a product for assessment by a variety of peers, adults, and experts.

Most mental models involve a mixture of beliefs. The most critical thing to remember about them is that they may have little to do with the statements we make to others. Most teachers would automatically say that they believe all children can learn, but if we observe what they do in the classroom, we see that their actions and decisions are not congruent with that articulated belief.

Following is an example of one way a mental model determines the teaching of mathematics.

> *Mike Fellows is a research mathematician who believes that the same questions that confound research professors at the university graduate level are appropriate dilemmas for elementary school children to study. He feels that the questions that challenge computer analysts and designers of artificial intelligence form the basis of broader questions that link mathematics to real life. While young children and graduate students may not approach the problems in the same way, Mike argues that there is a generic problem that each can deal with. One example he uses focuses on the smallest number of connections necessary to create a complex system. To translate this concept into a problem for third graders, we must create good examples. Examples include snowplowing paved streets for a community that has limited funds and in which every house must be connected by pavement at the lowest expense possible. Many of Mike's colleagues disagree with him.*

How do you react? What mental models lead you to agree or prevent you from agreeing with Mike's idea? Be honest with yourself. This is not a test.

Most teachers are not aware of the mental models that drive them. Because we have not examined our mental models openly—that is, we have not actively processed them—they continue to govern our thoughts and decisions without our knowledge. Our primary task is to develop appropriate and powerful mental models, which may mean we need to change. But changing mental models is not easy because any genuine attempt to shift a mental model results in some uncertainty.

Further Exploration: Testing Assumptions

Sometimes we find that our practice cannot overcome assumptions our students have:

> *Sam was teaching a class where he focuses on helping teachers access their own creativity. He noticed that some of his students were anxious about one of the assignments. The students were focusing on getting the procedures exactly right, whereas Sam wanted them to use their individual creativity. He realized that, by giving an example of one way for students to do the assignment, he had brought forth his students' hidden assumption. Students want to "do well." To them, "doing well" meant the assignment had to be done in the exact way Sam had given as a mere suggestion. They were looking for what they believed he wanted instead of using the assignment as a springboard to develop and showcase their own creativity.*

The three of us have identified a number of mechanistic assumptions–aspects of mental models—that a great deal of school practice suggests. What is interesting is how quickly and firmly students pick up on unstated assumptions, as evidenced in the example in Sam's class, especially when these unstated assumptions pervade the very essence of the educational process and school itself.

Which of the following do you assume or does your school practice reflect?

❑ We can control and largely manipulate outcomes.

❑ Testing is generally a good motivator for meaningful learning.

❑ Positive reinforcement controlled by others is a proven way to help children learn anything important.

❑ Subjects are best learned when separated and taught within discrete time periods.

❑ Memorization for tests is the most effective way for students to learn.

❑ The arts are for artists and have nothing to do with cognition.

❑ Physical movement is unrelated to learning.

❑ We can force students to engage in meaningful learning by threatening to punish them for misbehavior and poor performance or by spelling out a direct reward ahead of time.

❑ Learning has to be done individually.

❑ There is only one correct answer and one way to arrive at that answer.

❑ There is a straight cause-effect relationship between teacher contact and student learning.

❑ The sequence in which knowledge is to be acquired has a fixed and best order.

❑ By acquiring a set of incremental skills, students will automatically know how to read or to perform in complex ways.

❑ If students do not learn what we want them to learn, then something is wrong with the students.

❑ Acquiring understanding of concepts is a cognitive process unrelated to attitude and unshaped by emotion.

❑ Learning is primarily reflected in behavioral change we can observe in our classrooms.

❑ Students learn only when paying attention.

❑ Schools are the only or the primary places of learning.

❑ Memory always requires memorization.

❑ We can control and separate learning from social interaction.

❑ Once students have memorized the rules they will not misbehave.

The problem with these assumptions is they are not supported by current research about the way the brain/ mind engages in meaningful learning. In fact, educational practice based on these assumptions generally contributes to a lack of meaning-centered learning and teaching.

If a significant number of these beliefs reflects practices in our schools, and if they are not supported by neuroscientific research findings about learning, then we must begin changing the conditions in schools by changing our beliefs about learning.

Questions to Begin to Ask Yourself

What kind of learning happens without direct instruction?

What are some of the things students learn instantly?

How would we need to approach assessment to challenge learners without triggering a sense of helplessness?

What would be different in your school if everyone believed that all subjects could, and sometimes should, be combined and interconnected?

What would be different in your school if everyone believed that learning generally occurs over time, but sometimes slowly and sometimes quickly?

What would be different in your school if everyone believed that the real indicators of meaningful learning are often not apparent on a quantitatively measurable test?

What would be different in your school if everyone believed that emotions actually influence understanding?

What would be different in your school if everyone believed that understanding does not come from adding up incremental bits and pieces of knowledge but from engaging in projects and processes that generate a sense of completion from the very beginning?

What would be different in your school if everyone believed that teachers are not always right?

Your comments

A Change Process

One way to change the ways education is practiced is to change the ideas we hold about it. Once we are no longer bound by entrenched assumptions that permeate much of education, we are free to develop new ideas. This book is intended to open possibilities. As we begin to realize that teaching can be an art of its own and that learning involves a vast array of complex experiences, a whole new excitement takes place. We have the freedom to *be* educators.

We have included the Caines' brain/mind learning principles (chapter 3) and theory of learning and instruction (part 3) because your mental model needs to be grounded in up-to-date ideas about learning and practice. However, we have purposely not overloaded this book with scientific explanations. Rather, we have developed activities to help you experience what these principles feel like when they are put into practice. Once people have a feel for something, it is easier for them to generate their own ideas, expressions, and expertise. For the artist, technique is developed as a way to present an idea, not as an end in itself. Such development can also be true for educators. The possibilities for applying the ideas in this book are limitless.

We call this book *MindShifts* because the principles about the ways people learn contradict many of the underlying assumptions practiced in our schools today. Accepting these ideas requires us to begin shifting our mental models. Let's face it; we all know that changes in education need to take place. Many of the changes are social, political, and economic in nature. Others are organizational and structural. Still others involve ways in which we directly interact with students in places we call classrooms.

We invite you to test, examine, and explore the ideas and processes that follow. As you grasp the richness and complexity of the operations carried on in every learning brain/mind, you will be in a stronger position to make the changes needed to teach for deeper meaning.

We underrate our brain and our intelligence . . .
We are all capable of huge and unsuspected learning
accomplishments without effort.

3

How the Brain/ Mic Learns

I like to speculate that what the mind is is the flow of information as it moves among the cells, organs and systems of the body . . . the mind, then, is that which holds the network together, often acting below our consciousness, linking and coordinating the major systems and their organs in an intelligently orchestrated symphony of life.

—Candace Pert
Molecules of Emotion

All of those engaged in early childhood education must be able to ground their actions and decisions in current understandings about how children learn. The quest for understanding is being aided by the explosion of research in the neurosciences. There is so much research, however, and it can be interpreted in so many different ways and for so many different purposes, that we need a powerful and practical guide for our thinking. It is particularly important to integrate the brain research with information from other fields, because it is only when we test such research against the richness of broad human experience and multiple research fields that a clearer picture of human potential emerges.

We know, for instance, that signals in the brain are transmitted by nerve cells called *neurons*. A neuron is shaped roughly like a tree. The branches (called *dendrites*) at one end receive information, and the "trunk" and "roots" (called the *axon* and *axon spikes*) at the other end send information. There is virtually an unlimited number of potential connections between dendrites and axons of different neurons. One of the most exciting recent findings is that the number and strength of these connections are influenced by experience, a phenomenon called *plasticity*.

The brain research can show that plasticity exists and that rich experience is important for creating more neural connections. But it takes research from many fields, together with the practical experience of educators and others, to help us understand what kinds of experiences learners need. The brain research does not stand alone.

The Brain/Mind Learning Principles

The Caines' goal has been to synthesize research from many *disciplines* into a set of brain/mind learning principles to serve as a foundation for thinking about learning. The principles make room for new information from such fields as the neurosciences, cognitive psychology, stress theory, and creativity. The principles also include perspectives from the new sciences as well as what we know of the best of practice and the broader human experience. They are updated in this edition.

The most critical point about these principles is not only the research that supports each, but what education will look like if educators act with them in mind. Educators who believe in these principles will think, act, and make decisions in profoundly different ways from educators trained and educated with a behavioral or Industrial Age perspective.

1. The Brain Is a Living System

A system is a collection of parts that functions as a whole. Examples include clouds, rivers, trees, all of which function as parts of ecosystems. The brain meets this criterion beautifully. For instance, the amygdala has a great deal to do with emotions and the hippocampus with memory; although each region has its own function, the brain still operates as a whole, purposeful, and dynamic entity, with memory and emotion influencing each other.

A living system, in addition, has some specific properties that have a great bearing on how infants and young children function.

- The system seeks to survive and protect itself, as do infants who need food, comfort, shelter, and support.

- The system grows and adapts to its environment, as do infants who learn, change, and develop, all within the constraints of the places where they find themselves.

- Very small incidents can have vast and unexpected ramifications, as occurs when a single encounter generates cascades of emotions and responses, some of which can lead to consequences that last forever.

- The system is immensely resilient, and it can absorb relatively large inputs from the environment without noticeable consequence, as we find in those children who seem to rise beyond relatively troubled environments.

Other research shows that body, brain, and mind interact profoundly. For example, stress can weaken the immune system, and relaxation and laughter can strengthen it. We also know that children who learn to play the piano or sing in a choir improve their spatial reasoning and that learning to read enhances students' ability to think in abstractions. Everything that happens to us has both a direct and indirect effect due to the nature of the interconnectedness of the brain.

2. The Brain/Mind Is Social

Throughout our lives, the brain/mind changes in response to its engagement with others, so much so that individuals must always be seen as integral parts of larger social systems. Part of our identity depends on establishing community and finding ways to belong. As Darling (1996) notes, "For the first year or two of life outside the womb, our brains are in the most pliable, impressionable, and receptive state they will ever be in" (18). We begin to be shaped as the immensely receptive brain/mind interacts with our early environment and interpersonal relationships.

Neuroscientists have been able to document changes in infants' brain cells based upon very early interactions with adults. Daddy's smile and Aunt Agatha's "coochi coo" all appear to result in changes in how neurons communicate with each other (see Diamond and Hopson 1998). Even before children are born they appear to be sensitive to Mother's voice and heartbeat, and once born, they can identify and prefer her voice to any other female voice.

One capacity that is profoundly influenced by social interaction is language. Although we are all born with a predisposition to speak, the development of language is almost totally dependent on hearing others speak first and joining in with ever more appropriate sounds and movements. Every child is actually born with the potential to master every one of the more than five thousand languages and dialects, but it has been shown that children have begun to lose some of their flexibility and have even begun to acquire an accent by the time they are one year old. Lev Vygotsky (1978) suggests that even the ability for people to engage in internal dialogue—to think in their minds—is learned after experiencing external dialogue.

3. The Search for Meaning Is Innate

In general terms, the search for meaning refers to making sense of our experiences. Thus it involves our values and purposes and the questions that drive us, such as "Who am I?" and "Why am I here?" The search for meaning is survival oriented and basic to the human brain/mind. While the ways in which we make sense of our experience change over time, the central drive to do so is lifelong.

Every one of us is born with some basic biological equipment that allows us to make sense of the world. In fact, Restak (1995) says that the main purpose of the brain is to "make inner representations of reality" (3). Anyone who has ever lived through the "why" questions of young children or the seemingly endless curiosity of toddlers knows that children are born with an innate need to touch, smell, observe, listen to, and generally experience and figure out their world. The brain needs and automatically registers the familiar while simultaneously searching for and responding to novel stimuli. We are biologically programmed to make sense of our experience. In other words, we are innately motivated to search for meaning.

It seems as though there are two facets to this search for meaning. On the one hand, we are born to function as scientists, discovering what our world is about. On the other, we are born to function as artists, giving expression and voice to meanings that we create as we engage with life.

An emerging field in cognitive science called *theory theory* deals with our innate propensities to act as scientists. For example, Gopnik and Meltzoff (1997) argue convincingly that infants are born with the capacity to develop theories and hypotheses about how the world works. Even before they acquire language, they test their hypotheses and make predictions. Gopnik and Meltzoff give one example of very young infants watching a ball moving along a trajectory, then disappearing behind a screen. By following the infants' eye movements, the researchers note that the infants make predictions about where the ball will emerge, and seem surprised and confused when the ball emerges somewhere else. (Incidentally, this experiment contributed to evidence that many of the capacities Piaget spoke about seem to be present at birth, or develop much earlier and in different ways from the ways in which he described.)

4. The Search for Meaning Occurs through Patterning

The human brain/mind is not a formal logic machine. It is much better at making sense of life by finding patterns and order—something that science and art have in common. At the heart of patterning is categorization—finding similarities and differences and comparing and isolating features. We are all born with the ability to interpret the world around us by sorting its countless characteristics into categories. For example, we observe and sort lines, edges, and curves; light and dark; up and down; basic smells and tastes; and degrees of sound.

Our brains are even prewired with a basic number sense that gives very young infants a rudimentary awareness of the relationship among the numbers one through three. With experience, these abilities combine and gel into more complex categories such as "trees" and "people." Over time, richer and richer clusters of patterns take shape in our minds.

Of course, categories do not help much unless we can move around, so we are also innately equipped with the ability to develop maps of where we are in space and time (see principle 9). In fact, we also build a life map or story, which is how we maintain a sense of who we are.

Ultimately, the result of all this patterning is that humans construct mental models of reality. Then we perceive, relate to, and act on the world around us in terms of those categories, maps, and mental models. The educational philosophy of constructivism is about the creation of such perceptions and relationships.

Patterning is grounded in physiology. Groups of brain cells combine into neural networks that fire in the same ways consistently. Learning is required when an entrenched pattern is challenged or disrupted and new answers are needed. New experiences, meanings, and understandings reconfigure these automatic patterns. And such relearning often takes time because the changes are not just mental; they are physiological.

5. Emotions Are Critical to Patterning

Scientists' conception of the role emotions play in learning has vacillated. At times in the early part of the century, for example, emotions were largely ignored because the inner workings of the mind tended to be disregarded. Behaviorists were interested in observable, quantifiable phenomena and emotion. Since then, at least in the field of education, emotions have been treated as important but basically separate from thinking. Separating emotion from thinking has been the educational profession's way of acknowledging both while not effectively addressing the ways that they operate together.

In recent years, more and more researchers are seeing emotions as important, even in higher-order thinking. Researchers such as Joseph LeDoux in *The Emotional Brain* (1996) argue that there are different emotional circuits. He has done a great deal of work to trace the circuit for fear and its impact on our thinking. Antonio Damasio (1994) now says that thought and emotion cannot be separated, and that body and brain, including the emotions, form one indissociable unity. And another researcher, Candace Pert, who wrote *Molecules of Emotion* (1997), has shown that one reason for the unity of body and brain is that some of the chemical signals and carriers of information between neurons (neurotransmitters) are found throughout the body, not just in the neural circuits above our shoulders.

The bottom line is that emotion and cognition interact, energize, and shape each other. It is useful and appropriate, at times, to speak of them separately, but they are inseparable in the brains and experiences of learners. Thus Restack (1995) says that "almost every thought, no matter how bland, is accompanied by an emotion, no matter how subtle" (21).

One reason patterns are so hard to change is because of our emotional commitment to them. We are deeply invested in our assumptions and beliefs about others, be they parents, teachers, siblings, or friends. We are also invested in our individual beliefs about how the universe, our spiritual beliefs, and the world work. Changing these beliefs is not easy and can involve significant emotional volatility because they affect more than facts; they affect our sense of who we are.

6. Every Brain Simultaneously Perceives and Creates Parts and Wholes

Ultimately, there are two separate but simultaneous tendencies in all of us for organizing information. One is to reduce information to parts. The other is to perceive and work with information as a whole or series of wholes. These simultaneous tendencies spring from the organization of the brain.

Some evidence for the capacity to deal with both parts and wholes stems from split brain research. When the corpus callosum (the bundle of nerve fibers that links the left and right hemispheres of the brain) is severed in adults, it seems as though different capacities are housed in different sides of the brain. The research indicates that the left brain tends to be more verbal and analytical, while the right brain is more visual and intuitive. This split-brain research suggests that people tend to be analytical or intuitive. However, in people with an intact brain, both hemispheres work together and communicate via the corpus callosum so that our analytical and intuitive capacities are integrated.

The essential problem is that what constitutes a part and a whole is not always immediately obvious. For example, throwing a ball to a child may be a whole activity in one context, yet just part of a game in another. The key is to realize that life seems to be organized according to some natural wholes that the brain/mind recognizes very easily. These include stories, projects, puzzles, games, social events, relationships, and concepts. Thus, we perceive a whole puzzle even though we are focusing our attention on only one individual piece, and conversely, we can look at an entire puzzle and see the individual pieces that make it up.

Every event is processed in the brain as a complex experience that consists of larger wholes in which the parts are embedded and integrated. The brain/mind is designed to perceive both separateness and interconnectedness.

7. Learning Involves Both Focused Attention and Peripheral Perception

The core idea is that the brain/mind is immersed all the time in a field of sensations, images, and input, and continuously has to select what to attend to and what to ignore. Now attention itself is natural and tends to be driven by what is of most interest or relevance to the satisfaction of wants and needs.

However, even while paying direct attention, children are also absorbing information that lies beyond their immediate focus. This input ranges from basic background sensations (sound, color, chatter, laughter) to the behaviors and aspects of the environment that reflect the beliefs and practices of a culture. This dual operation of attention and peripheral perception occurs all the time in every context, including the home and the classroom. It is particularly important for infants who are literally being "programmed" by their context.

Much of this peripheral learning for older children and adults is seen in implicit memory (Schacter 1996). Let us say that you are in a room full of items. After you leave the room, you might not be able to recollect consciously everything that was there, and you might even swear that some named items were not there. And yet research shows that if experimenters give you the option to identify different items from a list, you are likely to choose those that were in the room, even if you never remember seeing them! Commercials work in the same way. Even if you see something only once or out of the corner of your eye, and argue vehemently that you did not see the name of the product, given a number of choices in a store you are likely to select or prefer the product you claim never to have seen.

The fact that we perceive peripherally has immense importance for education because it means that children in a school and at home are actually being profoundly influenced by the total environment. What are the colors saying to them? What messages are being conveyed by buildings designed like factories and prisons? How do they respond to bells? What of the impact of adults? How are students influenced by the media? And what is the impact of the content and emotional color of the actual conversations to which they are exposed? It is clear, for example, that body language and facial displays that signal respect or contempt, patience or impatience, confidence or insecurity, ignorance or expertise have an impact on the learner. That is why the design of the peripheral environment, and the state of mind and very "beingness" of the people in a school and house, all have an impact on how and what people actually learn.

8. Learning Always Involves Conscious and Unconscious Processes

Neuroscientists such as Joseph LeDoux (1996) are demonstrating that the unconscious is real. The processes of the "cognitive unconscious span many levels of mental complexity, all the way from the routine analysis of the physical features of stimuli by our sensory systems to remembrance of past events to speaking grammatically to imagining things that are not present, to decision making, and beyond" (29). A great deal of the insights we have and the patterns that we grasp are a consequence of ongoing unconscious processing.

Psychologists have also known for a long time that understanding is largely a consequence of deep processing. Thus, complex learning depends on a person's capacity to take charge of the processing of experience, which is a matter of becoming aware of what is actually happening.

As we get older, we have the opportunity to develop mindfulness. In the words of Thich Nhat Hanh (1976), "'mindfulness' refers to 'keeping one's consciousness alive to the present reality'" (11). Ellen Langer (1989) notes that being aware of what is actually happening is different from mindlessly moving though life. When we are mindless we are locked into what Langer calls "category traps," or static ways of thinking and perceiving. We all experience this automaticity to some extent in the routines that we get into, say, in our driving, in our relationships with the same people over a long period of time, or in the ways in which we are programmed as described in principle 7. We "squeeze" reality—our actions and thoughts—into those fixed categories. Despite all our intellectual learning, many of our underlying beliefs and assumptions remain the same and are the invisible forces that keep us in a box.

It is by bringing to conscious awareness our assumptions, beliefs, habits, and practices that we begin to take charge of them and of our own learning and performance. In young children, it is usually necessary for an adult to mediate their experience so that they can become aware. An example is a child who doesn't like being splashed by paint but who has not registered that she has a choice to move away. As we grow older, we have the capacity to develop awareness and to engage in metacognitive observation. The more we can observe our thinking, the more we can self-regulate and take charge of our own learning.

9. We Have at Least Two Ways of Organizing Memory

When we think of memory we automatically think of what we have "stored" and can "retrieve." But it isn't that simple because memory is also naturally working all the time in the present moment as we move around in the world and try to make sense of our contexts and our experiences. Stored memories would be useless if we could not call upon them as needed, and what determines need is our moment-to-moment context. It is the context, that is, the need of the moment, that determines when or why we pull a particular name out of storage and when we bring to mind facts about automobiles and finance.

O'Keefe and Nadel's (1978) model is the most useful and effective because it deals with this core difference between static and dynamic memory. They point out that we all have some systems in which static information is stored. These include some of the systems that cognitive scientists have identified, such as declarative memory (facts), semantic memory (meanings), procedural memory (skills), and emotional memory (feelings). All of these systems can be described as taxon systems (from *taxonomies*). These systems can be programmed independently or programmed through experience, which is why it is possible to learn by rote facts, vocabulary, spelling words independent of a living context, and why programmed, isolated emotional responses can become the basis of "mindless" behaviors, or in extreme cases, phobic responses executed independent of "rational" expectations.

On the other hand, each of us also has a locale (from *location*), experiential system that registers and organizes moment-to-moment events in life. The regions of the brain that are most important for our locale system to operate are the hippocampus and prefrontal lobes. According to neuroscientists, this system is designed to register where we are in space and to register the unfolding story of what happens to us. Hence it is essentially an ongoing autobiographical system that constructs moment-to-moment, meaningful maps of the world. It calls to mind and indexes the variety of things that we see, hear, feel, and experience at any one time, while we simultaneously talk to people and go about our business. Thus the locale system is referred to as a *dynamic system.*

Some taxon systems, particularly those that store emotional memories, are fully functioning at birth. However, the locale memory system develops over time, which is why very young children cannot fully integrate their experiences; that is, in the early years, infants and babies can store many impressions and routines, but the connections take time to develop.

The emerging message is clear: The brain, with its complex architecture and limitless potential, is a highly plastic, constantly changing entity that is powerfully shaped by our experiences in childhood and throughout life.

—Marion Diamond and
Janet Hopson
Magic Trees of the Mind

10. Learning Is Developmental

Brain development and learning are two sides of the same coin. The physical structure does not just grow because it is fed and sheltered. The life experiences that a person has literally lead to new connections between neurons and the secretion of chemicals that transmit signals.

There do seem to be stages in the physical development of the brain. In the first three years after birth, for instance, the rate of growth is prodigious as a great many new connections are made. Within this period, the capacity to experience emotions is much more developed than the capacity to think. Even up to puberty, the brain shows tremendous fluidity and capacity for change. This fluidity is one reason why "windows of opportunity," or key times for learning, are so important. It is much easier to learn a second language in the first few years of life, for instance, than after puberty. We should add that brain growth and development continue throughout life and that some capacities (such as long-term planning) mature only in the second and third decades.

One key for educators is that all learning builds on what has gone before. We build and expand on prior knowledge. We also interpret new experiences and new ideas in terms of what we have previously experienced or come to understand. For example, new categories are developed by building on those that are already in place. Lakoff and Johnson (1980) point out that we are born with the capacity to recognize *up* and *down,* and *in* and *out,* and by using metaphors, much more complex ideas develop. We can talk about being at the top or bottom of a hierarchy or belonging to the inner circle.

How much any infant or adult can learn is open to question. However, we do know that, with the exception of those who get diseases that stop learning, everyone can learn throughout life, and that we can all almost certainly learn much more than we or most others think we can.

11. Complex Learning Is Enhanced by Challenge and Inhibited by Threat Associated with a Sense of Helplessness or Fatigue

In The Emotional Brain, Joseph LeDoux (1996) shows our response to fear by explaining that we have two separate response systems. He calls them the "high road" (a relatively slow system) and the "low road" (a relatively fast system). We simplify his discussion here in the interest of brevity. He shows that sensory information comes into our thalamus where we form a very crude impression of our experience. If fear is not triggered, information goes primarily to the sensory cortex, which refines the sensory input and clarifies what it is we are seeing, hearing, or experiencing. Simultaneously, the amygdala forms emotional responses in accordance with what has happened. Such a response is LeDoux's high road. However, if the first crude impression indicates something to fear, signals are sent primarily to the amygdala without going via the sensory cortex, and the fight or flight response is triggered immediately. LeDoux calls this the low road. Using Hart's term, we call this low-road response *downshifting.*

Although LeDoux deals directly with fear, there is evidence from many other sources that downshifting is not caused just by fear itself. The low road is triggered by fear related to a sense of helplessness or to fatigue. In these circumstances we revert to more primitive or early programmed responses and lose access to higher brain functioning, just as LeDoux describes.

Very young children *are* helpless and lack the capacity to take charge of their responses or their experience. Consequently they can be programmed very easily into a state of constant fear, which is why we must take such care to avoid overstimulation and abandonment.

The alternative to downshifting is self-efficacy, or the exercise of personal agency. We can foster self-efficacy simply by supporting and encouraging the learning that students are already disposed to do (such as learning to speak and walk). In addition, self-efficacy develops when children have genuine opportunities to make decisions and choices within a safe environment.

12. Every Brain Is Uniquely Organized

We all have the same set of systems, and yet we are all different. The factors that make us the same are precisely those that allow us to be different. For example, we are all born with about one hundred billion neurons. But our genetic blueprint, coupled with unique experiences, means that each of us will have wiring that differs in many ways from that of everyone else. We all have all the same senses, but by virtue of our different environments and different genetic makeup, the input for our senses differs to some extent from that of everyone else who has ever lived or will ever live. In addition, while we all have a social and cultural background, they vary enormously and influence the perceptual filters that we develop. We all perceive the world in different ways and act according to the way that we perceive it. So we create realities that have much in common with the realities of others, yet each is unique.

However, it is critical to see that every human being is also a unique system. An educator or parent who has a grasp of systems features sees that a style or even "disability" is always a part of a more complex, whole person. We do not deal adequately with children if we focus simply on specific styles or abilities. We have to understand how to treat the whole child so that our students have opportunities to engage specific abilities.

Uniqueness is a fact of life. Race, color, creed, and culture all are aspects of individuality, but even within a culture in which all people are overtly similar, immense differences exist. Nature is diverse and in fact thrives on diversity. The idea of only one kind of flower or tree or bird is as ridiculous as one kind of human being.

Being open and being attentive is more effective than being judgmental. This is because people naturally tend to be good and truthful when they are being received in a good and truthful manner.

John Heider, *The Tao of Leadership*

4

The Mindshifts Process Groups

Our goal is to assist people to examine and change their own mental models and to apply the changes to the classroom and school. Actually, we have four ongoing goals:

- developing a learning community
- internalizing a theory of learning
- developing the habits and skills of reflection
- developing a sense of orderliness and process

Meeting these goals means that participants will be engaged in personally meaningful learning, and for such learning to happen, they must implement the elements of brain-based teaching, more fully described in chapter 19:

1. The participants need to feel safe and engaged; they must experience a state of relaxed alertness to change.

2. The participants must be immersed in the sorts of complex experiences that are appropriate for them and in which the material to be learned is embedded.

3. The participants must actively process those experiences to learn from them.

What are the sources of order? How do we create organizational coherence, where activities correspond to purpose? How do we create structures that move with change, that are flexible and adaptive, even boundaryless, that enable rather than constrain? How do we simplify things without losing both control and differentiation? How do we resolve personal needs for freedom and autonomy with organizational needs for prediction and control?

—Margaret J. Wheatley
Leadership and the New Science

Our research and experience indicate that the most important first step is for you to create a sense of community in your classroom. Adults working together on their professional development must also take this first step. While we all have to do our own learning, the brain is a social brain, and it is extremely beneficial to be able to learn together.

One of the most effective ways to help individuals and systems change—a way that encourages brain-based learning—is to develop small groups. We flesh out the details in chapter 5, but we introduce the foundations of the process here. Take some care in setting up your groups.

Whom the Groups Suit

The groups are suitable for any adult who works in or with a school or larger educational or professional unit. Most commonly, participants are teachers and administrators. However, we have seen and invited the participation of special resource personnel, librarians, psychologists, secretaries, custodians, and teacher aids. We have also used this process in businesses. And we encourage parents to participate.

We suggest including all adults in a school because every adult contributes to the creation of the community for the children, and children learn from every adult. For instance, the atmosphere in the school office and that on the playground set much of the tone for the experiences that students have in school. The objective is for all adults to have a common mental model of how people learn, then to develop brain-based ways to do their work. Our own experience is that groups function best when they begin with participants most of whom do not work very closely together. Variety and novelty of input expand our horizons. Of course, as your group progresses, participants will get to know one another quite well.

Volunteers

It is essential that group participants be volunteers to ensure psychological safety. Participants need to risk some personal disclosure. People are at various developmental stages in their professional growth, and individual strengths and weaknesses become apparent. In such circumstances, it is vital that the people who engage in the process do so willingly.

Ensuring that all participants are volunteers may be difficult, especially if some people feel pressured to participate and only pretend to volunteer. However, such pressure is likely to sabotage the process and lead to discomfort. Our advice is that you make it clear during the first few meetings that no one should feel pressured to participate and that you will not tolerate someone pressuring another. However, there is nothing wrong with noting that those who choose to participate are likely to find that they have embarked on a challenging, deeply fulfilling personal and professional growth process.

Group Size

The ideal number of participants is about seven to twelve. When you have more than twelve people, there may not be enough time for participants to express individual thoughts and opinions. When the number falls below seven, the energy may drop off and there will not be enough variety of opinions. There may be reasons for the group to be larger or smaller. We suggest you practice the process in the way we recommend before you experiment with other sizes.

Forming Groups

There is no one right way to get started. One or two teachers may read *Making Connections* and decide that they want to form a group. A school or district may have an inservice on brain-based learning, and a principal or curriculum director may organize groups to apply these ideas. A school may embark on a long-term restructuring program and the staff may vote to use the Mindshifts process. A small group or track may form a group, then explain it to others whose curiosity is aroused by seeing the results. We have also seen administrators from several areas form a group. The principle requirement is that participants have an idea of their reasons for forming a group, whether they read, informally discuss, or attend a formal inservice.

Location

As the purpose of the group is to engage in reflective learning and avoid being caught up in everyday issues, we suggest that you meet away from your normal place of work to reduce the number of reminders about work and the number of interruptions. You might meet in an office or a part of the school or district where you seldom find yourselves.

On occasion, it is simply not possible to meet outside the place of work. In those circumstances, simply choose a place that enables you to function peacefully and comfortably, and uninterrupted as much as possible. Be sure to allow for some transitional time that allows participants to finish the business of the day and focus on the group in a fresh way.

Sometimes groups like to meet in private homes. Should you choose to do so, we suggest you rotate and take turns being a host and a guest. We also strongly suggest that you not regard this time as one during which you have to entertain people or go out of your way to provide a great deal of food and drink.

Time and Duration

We recommend that you meet once a week for two hours, although doing so is not always possible. In the first school where we attempted this process, it became obvious that meetings could be held only three times a month for about one-and-a-half hours. This schedule worked very well for this group. However, fewer, shorter meetings will probably not provide the depth and richness of experience that our recommendations provide.

Facilitators

It is appropriate and important for someone whom the participants accept and who has good process skills to lead the overall proceedings for some weeks or months.

However, the goal is for everyone to be leader and follower. Meeting this goal is critical to establish mutual respect and to overcome the tendency for social and professional status to interfere with genuine communication. Some aspects of leadership should rotate on a regular basis. Different people might be responsible for facilitating different aspects of the group meeting each week, while one person remains responsible for the whole.

Similarly, when groups launch informally, without outside facilitation, we would expect natural leaders to take charge in the early stages. However, we strongly recommend that leadership of some processes begin to rotate fairly soon.

What the Group Does

There are three primary phases for each group meeting. The first phase is an ordered sharing, which develops a learning atmosphere and establishes the basic conditions for an effective group. The second is reflective study of the brain/mind learning principles, which is at the heart of internalizing the theory of brain-based learning. The third is an exploration of the practical implications of the theory. See figure 4-1 for the amount of time each should take. Such exploration helps you implement your learning in your work. Ultimately, the three phases become a platform for personal and shared experimentation, peer coaching, action research, further study, and system change.

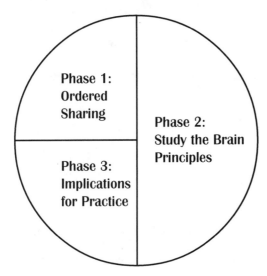

Figure 4-1. Time blocks for each phase

Phase 1: Ordered Sharing

The objective of this phase is for each person to express a personal opinion about some big idea. Each person has roughly the same amount of time to speak, and everyone participates. No one is judged or debated because every opinion is simply heard and valued. The ordered sharing allows for the development of a sense of order, continuity, and momentum. Choose a timekeeper for this process. Make sure that everyone has an equal opportunity to be the timekeeper. Following are the steps of this phase.

1. **Sit in a closed circle at equal heights.** It may be tempting for some people to sit on the floor and for you to simply arrange yourselves in convenient clusters. However, we strongly suggest that you sit at roughly equal heights (using comfortable chairs where possible) and that you attempt to form a circle. The circle is part of what it takes to form coherence and eliminate hierarchy and competitiveness.

2. **Examine your core material.** The core material for this phase is one very brief but very big idea. We use what we call "principles of connectedness":

   - Everything is separate and connected.

   - What is, is always in process.

   - Reality consists of matter, energy, and meaning.

   - Order is present everywhere.

   - Inner and outer reflect each other.

   - The whole is greater than the sum of its parts.

   - Everything comes in layers.

   - Everything is both part and whole simultaneously.

   - Reality is both linear and nonlinear.

   - Rhythms and cycles are present everywhere.

- Stable systems resist change; dynamic systems exist by changing.

- The whole is contained in every part.

The ideas should be general enough to generate many possible meanings and many personal experiences. There are no right or wrong responses. You will also find that, over time, the ideas help you rethink the nature of curriculum and what an integrated curriculum is really all about.

After the first three months you might begin to explore other material. The material you choose should always have the quality of being expansive and nondidactic, but it does not have to be verbal. You might like to play some short excerpt from a great symphony, examine a great work of art or a photograph, go outside and look at the sunset, read a brief excerpt from some great poetry or philosophy.

3. **Express personal opinions.** Once any volunteer expresses a personal opinion about the chosen subject, the person to the left is next to speak. There is no magic to whether you go right or left. The key is to be consistent. The expression of personal opinions continues around the circle. Keep a time limit of, perhaps, one or two minutes. Because you allow each person an opportunity to speak and be heard, there is no competition for time.

   Participants may comment about anything that is sparked by the big idea, ranging from a personal anecdote to a philosophical speculation. They are not obligated to follow from or add to what someone else has said. Each person has the floor and is totally in charge of what to talk about. If someone says something that another was going to talk about, and that point is still uppermost in mind, the second person is free to talk about it. The key is to refrain from agreeing with or criticizing another. Do *not* say, "I think X was right" or "I disagree with Y." If you do want to springboard from another's thoughts, say something such as, "The idea or story about . . . is interesting. In my opinion . . ."

4. **Refrain from interrupting.** No one comments or responds to what individuals say while they are speaking. There is neither opposition nor support. In fact, as much as possible, participants avoid gestures or body language that convey an opinion, such as nodding heads. Every silent member pays full attention to what the speaker is saying. Feel free to nod your head in affirmation during all the *other* phases of the group process.

5. **The timekeeper monitors timing and participation.** The timekeeper ensures that no one exceeds the time limit. When the time has expired, the timekeeper says "time" or "process." The speaker may complete a sentence, but does not get more time to elaborate.

   Some participants may not want to say anything. We strongly encourage all to say something, even if it is very brief, rather than to pass. Nonparticipation by a few can deflate others.

We know that the process may seem counterintuitive at first. It is designed to be so as the objective is to change some of our customary modes of communication. The process erases hierarchy and status differences. It also begins to build a deeper mode of listening. In the early stages, some people might feel pressure, particularly those waiting for their turn. The pressure diminishes after a few sessions, particularly when it becomes evident that you do *not* have to find something original to say.

Phase 2: Study the Brain Principles

Spend some time in reflective study of the brain-based principles. The purpose is to explore the core ideas and procedures, and to relate them to your personal experience. The goal is also to see how the principle operates in your life and relates to your own learning. This book summarizes the theory and explains the brain/mind principles in chapter 3. One chapter is also devoted to each of the brain/mind learning principles, including a large number of activities and questions for you to explore to understand each principle further.

You might also read *Making Connections: Teaching and the Human Brain* while you work through this book. *Making Connections* is the foundation upon which *MindShifts* and our work in schools are based. It recounts the initial research that led to the formation of the principles and describes the Caine theory of brain-based learning and teaching.

In a one-and-a-half-hour meeting, this phase occupies about forty-five to sixty minutes. There is no need to use ordered sharing during this phase. People are free to interact and engage in lively discussion. However, maintain the spirit of the ordered sharing: listen fully and give one another adequate opportunities to participate.

There is also a core dynamic that is extremely important. The goal of this phase is to examine ideas in light of personal experiences, which means that you constantly explore some relevant event in your life, then relate it to brain-based learning theory to personalize the theory. There are several skills—aspects of active processing—that the group might like to explore. They will assist you with your learning and later with your teaching.

Active Listening

Pay full attention and ask questions that enable the speaker to clarify thoughts.

Inner Listening

Listen to yourself to become aware of your mental models and hidden assumptions. One key is to recognize that, whenever you have a strong emotional response to an idea or behavior, that response reflects a deep belief. It is important to refrain from judging your beliefs, however. Change occurs when and if you are ready. The goal here is increased awareness.

Phase 3: Implications for Practice

The goal of this phase is to use the group process as a platform for a deeper inquiry into the nature of education and your professional role in it. At the end of each chapter on the brain/mind learning principles is a series of questions that relate the principle to your work. Spend at least 15 minutes in each meeting exploring these questions. However, do not rush to change what you do. Rather, over time, other questions and issues might arise. You might find yourself beginning to test and experiment with other strategies and processes with colleagues, which is a natural development.

Maintain the Process

In this chapter we describe some of the process principles that will make your group effective. Remember that it is the nature of the process that matters most. Everything should be done with that attitude. It is very easy for a group to turn into an orthodox group that studies particular strategies or researches a particular issue or problem. Study and research are fine, and can be incorporated into a process group. But it is the spirit of the process itself that is vital for authentic listening and dynamic learning.

Nurturing the Larger System

When two or more groups form in one school, we suggest that the separate groups meet together every six weeks to share and reflect on their process group experiences. In this way, the larger system can benefit from the spirit and learning that take place in the small-group sessions.

Action

Before forming your Mindshifts process groups, you might like to take some time to try the ordered sharing. Our experience has been that it takes two or three trials before you become comfortable with the process. Once you have somewhat of a feel for it, we suggest you form groups that will meet regularly. Again, however, our experience indicates that it may take from one to three weeks before the membership of the group stabilizes.

A Final Word

There is always more. How long should a group continue?
When do groups change membership and focus? How do
new groups form? How does one integrate the process into
the larger system? What is the developmental path for
educators? These and other questions will be answered in
part with experience and in part through learning from
others. We deal with some of the issues in our other
writings. We also do video or live conferences on the
Internet for process groups, so feel free to contact us. We
have a chat room, and we invite you to share your learning
with us at Cainelearning.com.

5

Additional Guidance on the Nature of Process

"What is REAL?" asked the Rabbit one day . . . "Real isn't how you are made," said the Skin Horse. "It's a thing that happens to you. When a child loves you . . . then you become Real."

—Margery Williams
The Velveteen Rabbit

The Mindshifts process groups are not ordinary study groups. They require a spirit, a philosophy grounded in the brain/mind learning principles and a designed process.

Principles of Process

As will become clear, one purpose of the small group is to generate a new rhythm for communicating and learning. A learning community needs spontaneity and routine, constancy and becoming.

To that end, the following steps are very important:

1. Create a Psychologically Safe Environment

Groups must be psychologically safe so participants can feel genuinely free to test their own beliefs and assumptions, and to risk exploring their thinking and their practices in front of others. We want to reiterate that, to create a sense of safety, participants must be volunteers. The best way to sabotage the effectiveness of a group is to force people to be a part of it when they do not want to be, then to demand that they change. Such demands are almost guaranteed to cause them to downshift (a discussion of downshifting occurs later). Participants should also commit aloud to the group to keeping in confidence everything shared by all other participants; no discussion or statement will be made public without the consent of the person who shared it. Deciding whether or not to participate in a group is a delicate process. A basic requirement is trust. It will take some time for people to decide whether someone's professions of commitment are genuine, so you should expect to have a few meetings during which people gauge how safe the group really is.

2. Maintain a Consistent Routine

Although the brain/mind loves novelty, it must have a degree of routine and consistency. It begins to anticipate regular events. You can use routine to set the stage for your learning and to build a good climate in the group. In general, set aside time for each of the following.

Preliminaries

Get your venting out of the way. While the daily pressures of teaching can often be frustrating, the group process should not be used for venting frustration. Repeated venting may dissipate the energy needed for positive change. We suggest that if the need to vent your feelings about the day is strong, then do so briefly before your group begins the actual Mindshifts process.

A Way to Begin

You could start each meeting with, say, a minute of total and restful silence. Or begin with some relatively brief relaxation exercise, which might range from stretching to listening to music.

A Way to End

There are two components that we find very useful. First, take a moment to reflect on what happened and what you learned from this group experience. We suggest that each person in turn briefly share some personal insight. This process is not a time for competition, discussion, or debate, but merely a time to share. Second, close with a simple ceremony. A song is one possibility, a moment of silence another, a "football huddle" a third. For the last, you stand in a circle, then together say aloud "one, two, three" and clap.

3. Maintain the Group Energy

The group process has very specific parameters. Some may be uncomfortable with the parameters, but we have found that the process is most effective when groups adhere to them. Energy dissipates very quickly if people come and go when they wish. Hence all members of your group should agree and adhere to a starting and finishing time. Start each meeting on time, even if everyone has not yet arrived. Late arrivals should wait for a break in the process before joining the group.

4. Stay or Go, but Don't Come and Go

As the group process is for volunteers, members should feel free either to participate or drop out. However, groups need to develop a sense of community, rhythm, and safety, which is almost impossible if people come and go. After the group has begun meeting regularly, someone may wish to drop out or join, which is fine. However, after the first few meetings, don't allow new members to join or exmembers to rejoin. At this stage, it is not a time to be nice or to please or appease people.

5. Slow Down to Speed Up

There is often a great temptation to "cover" material quickly. Covering material is not the thrust of this process. Depth is more important, just as it is in our teaching. Sound learning theory reveals that much learning is unconscious, and that what we learn is organized around what is profoundly important to us. The goal of the groups is to give people time to explore what is important to them and to give their brains and minds time to digest what they are considering. You need to spend some time reflecting deeply on the nature of your own ideas about learning and teaching; you also need to feel free and safe enough to take risks and experiment. The learning you experience now will be the foundation and platform for changing what you do in your teaching. This approach may seem counterintuitive and slow to begin with. In the long run, however, it will allow members to go deeper to significant learning, which is the driving force of the groups. You will actually achieve deep learning in less time if you take it slowly than if you try to hurry it.

6. Avoid Having a Specific View of the "Good" Professional in Mind

A developmental path exists in all professions. In that sense we do have outcomes in mind as a consequence of this process. However, our two basic initial goals are for members to internalize a theory of learning and to develop some particular reflective habits and skills. As you develop these skills and begin to apply what you learn to your profession, you will make some mindshifts naturally; such shifts will be reflected in changes in your teaching practice. Such changes, ultimately, are what will lead you to teach more effectively. However, it is critical in the early stages of this process that you do not have *specific* student results or goals in mind.

7. Benefit from Individual Differences

The group will consist of people with various beliefs, goals, styles, roles, and functions. Such diversity will be invaluable in the long run because it contributes to a wide variety of input, attitudes, and ideas that will greatly increase your understanding. However, the differences can also be frustrating. Some people, for example, like details; others like the big picture. Both attitudes are important; extremes of either are counterproductive. We suggest that one function of the group process be to explore individual differences. This exploration will help you understand other members and enable you to appreciate and adhere to the guidelines that really are important to the process.

You might choose to use one of the many instruments available such as the Myers-Briggs Type Indicator. Feel free to use such an instrument or profile, and to discuss various characteristics that may be the basis for individual differences. Indeed, you could explore this topic from time to time during your meetings. You will gain enormous insight into your students and their learning styles as well as into yourself, your colleagues, and members of the community.

8. Do Not Give Advice

You will probably be enormously tempted to tell one another what to do. However, giving direction or telling others what to do is *not* what your group is about. The goal is for people to learn from their own experiences, which is what the search for meaning is all about. Of course, sometimes you may want advice, and you may ask for it. Ask the person to stop if you don't like the advice he or she is giving. And be very careful about asking for advice during your group process as this can frustrate your own learning, even if advice is what you want. This area is a particular temptation for facilitators who might want to "guide" participants in their growth or solve problems for them. In the Mindshifts process, it is essential to allow members to create the conditions that develop their own awareness and to avoid trying to learn or solve their problems for them. Developing a unique awareness and solving one's own problems become a foundation for self-efficacy.

9. Maintain the Process

At times people may feel euphoric. At other times they may feel low. You may even reach a point where nothing seems to be happening or you have strong personal doubts about the process. Such mood changes are part of life. They are also quite natural when we are working to change our mental models. However, one function of the group is to develop a continuity of learning and a powerful sense of community, no matter what you are feeling. Such continuity and power will help you change.

Cautions

The Mindshifts process is not just about acquiring information. It is a way to learn about ourselves. Thus, it may become quite personal. Accordingly, there are several elements to bear in mind.

1. **We are not prescribing a process to use in classrooms.** This process is for you. Our purpose has been to develop a process for adults who volunteer to change. We make no recommendations whatsoever about how you might apply what you learn through this process in your classes with your students. Such a decision is a matter for your own judgment. However, the process is extremely powerful and is based on the brain/mind principles. It can be of great value as a model to assess your teaching and can provide you with ideas for what to do when working with students.

2. **Conflict resolution.** With the best intentions in the world, people sometimes find themselves in conflict. Sometimes two members may want to proceed in different directions or may have more fundamental differences about such issues as safety and privacy. If group members are unwilling to follow the guidelines, it may be better for them not to be involved. However, we also suggest that, should the need arise, you invest some time (including group time) in developing appropriate procedures to resolve conflicts.

The very participation in this process will change the climate in a school or environment. When students see us deeply engaged in our own learning, we send a message to all students that learning is natural, important, and on-going. Thus, part of the process of building a learning community is simply to be one.

Some Questions to Ponder

Someone once said that the extensive need for police, security cameras, and broad-based disciplinary action is a sign of a dysfunctional community. What would a healthy community look like?

What thoughts come to mind about the process suggestions described in this chapter? Have you experienced any similar principles and practices elsewhere? What underlying philosophy of change is suggested by the principles?

PART 2

Principles of Brain/Mind Learning

It is the letting go that is difficult.

The questions and concepts and knowledge of a lifetime

Hang on to me as the tether of a Bungi cord.

I want my expansion to be unimpaired,

The magnet to the Earth's center unimpeded.

Then truth can be known.

—Sam Crowell

The whole is greater than the sum of its parts.

6

The Brain Is a Living System

Imagine yourself sitting on a swing in a garden under a large tree. You are reading a book that is both exciting and emotionally involving, and your brain and body are totally engrossed. Your visual thalamus is taking in the information from the page and surroundings, sending it to your visual cortex where it is further processed in other areas of the limbic system and multiple areas of the cortex. The hippocampus is aiding in creating a map of what you are reading and translating the text into pictures. The hippocampus and prefrontal lobes are participating in pulling your outer reality in the garden and your inner world into a coherent map of experience. Your amygdala is mediating the emotions you feel and, along with a great variety of other organs, is continually responding to any unusual sounds or potential dangers. And depending on your general state of health, the state of your nervous system and of your own ongoing interpretation of events around you, ligands in the form of neurotransmitters, steroids, and peptides are communicating by passing complex messages to receptor sites located on brain cells, cells within your immune system and cells throughout your body. An immense and complex network of activity (of which you know little but without which you could not have this simple, pleasurable experience of sitting in a garden reading a book) is engaged.

The time has come for educators to understand the capacities of learners in fundamentally new ways. More specifically, the time has come to think in terms of what it is possible for people to be and to become, rather than simply in terms of how well they memorize facts and acquire skills. At every moment and in every situation a person is growing primarily as a human being, even though we may think that we are just teaching reading, math, or science.

The purpose of this chapter is to provide an overview of how complex the brain/mind is and to place learning within the context of the whole person. This principle, therefore, is an umbrella for the others, which explore more specific aspects of brain/mind functioning.

In the human brain/mind, most things are not linear—that is, single-directional or proportional—and responses are never totally predictable. The core fact is that body, brain, and mind form a single, interactive unity in which everything is connected in multiple ways to everything else. As Damasio (1994) notes, "The organism constituted by the brain-body partnership interacts with the environment as an ensemble, the interaction being of neither the body nor the brain alone" (87–88). This unity (which we call a *living system*) is not like a machine. We can't isolate one part and "fix it" without having an impact on many other parts. At the outset, therefore, we need to keep in mind some basic properties of the system.

In some ways we can compare this system to a city. In a city, there are always many things happening at one time. Utilities are operating. The media are at work. Government, education, business, and transport are functioning, even though there may be times of high and low activity. Our brains/minds are equally active, with a vast number of simultaneous processes taking place. Following are some basic characteristics that make the brain/mind a living system:

- **There is an innate urge in every person to grow and to connect.**
  Every living system seeks to expand and to grow—to become more. For humans, this desire to grow

means that we naturally strive to use more of our brains. Maslow called this striving the urge to self-actualize. We see growth and development in the way that plants move from seed to fruition, that animals, including humans, move from birth to maturity. We should add that although much of human growth is biologically predictable, who we become as people and how we develop our talents are ultimately open and the result of many factors that we cannot predict.

- **The system can be influenced—and partially programmed—but it cannot be controlled.**
  There are always multiple responses and capacities for action within the system. We can't just teach it one thing or treat just one aspect of behavior without creating a cascade (often invisible) of other effects. A smiley sticker, for example, can teach things about pleasing others and about power, control, and perfection.

- **Each of us is constantly adapting to our entire context.**
  Nothing that we experience is perceived in isolation. Thus, each child adjusts and adapts to her or his perception of school and also decides how school does or does not relate to life. Whenever we set out to "teach" kids, they experience a complex event that isn't registered just in the neocortex as information—there are sensory and emotional layers of processing that result in physiological changes that also influence and determine what a child will ultimately register. In any lesson or session, children always ask filtering questions such as the following:

  - Do I want to learn this?
  - Do I like doing this?
  - Do I like this place?
  - Does this mean anything to me?
  - Can I do this?
  - Do I respect this teacher?
  - Can I trust him or her?

They are all legitimate questions the brain/mind asks, and kids will answer them in some way. Most of this filtering is automatic, without a person being aware of what happened. Yet much depends on how the questions are framed and answered because the brain/mind will organize itself and deal with the incoming information accordingly.

The bottom line is that human beings decide what to do on the basis of purposes that have meaning to us. Human beings are adaptive; we respond to an ever-changing environment. Human beings are dynamical—we respond to our environment in ways that cannot be directly predicted because they are not based on clear, mechanistic, linear, cause-effect connections. Human beings learn.

Gaining a Sense of the Whole Child as a Living System

Being human means that the mind continually shifts and changes based on what is happening in its outer and inner worlds in the form of experiences. Anyone who has ever observed a child figure out how to play a game and become bored with it, then observed the boredom disappear as something in the child's thinking or imagination spurs her on to add a new twist to the game has seen something machines cannot do.

 ### Activity 1: Every Living System Strives to Grow and to Define Itself

Growth

Take some time to think about the times in your life when you have had an urge to do more with your life, to try something new, to become more proficient, to raise your standards.

From where did this urge come?

How did you deal with it?

Did it seem natural?

Can you remember feeling it as a young child?

Do you still feel it now?

I wish I could still draw. When I was in grammar school I used to draw decently. I loved to draw in pencil and chalk. Art of all kinds intrigues me, I also love music, and painting, and carpentry, and metalwork, and dancing, and sewing, and embroidering. I want to dance in my own ballet class, play my clarinet, and draw thousands of pictures. Really good ones. Create beautiful poems, cook and sew for my children, decorate my home, have a good marriage, be an active volunteer, go to church, be an astrophysicist, go to Mars and understand all my questions about life. That's not too much to ask, is it?

—An eleven-year-old, courtesy of Stephanie Pace Marshall

Commentary

A classroom and a school are environments within which the child's urge to grow and create can be nurtured and cultivated. Yet research shows that the higher students climb through the grade levels, the less creative they become. Our task is to respect and support the natural urge on the part of children to become more. The curriculum and instruction need to be geared to and organized around the propensity to grow and create. Unfortunately, perhaps, growth and creativity are messy and nonlinear, which means we have to find out how to create the dynamical, messy, semiorganized conditions in which people can flourish.

Self-Protection

A living system seeks to protect its sense of self. It may seem strange to think of ourselves as being protective, but we are. We need food, shelter, and companionship. We don't like to be unjustly accused. We avoid pain and what we regard as inappropriate danger. We look for a reasonable degree of stability and comfort. And, of course, we each do so in our own way.

Spend some time discussing different times and places in your life where you recognize that much of your effort was directed toward protecting yourself. Specifically reflect on the ways that you thought and felt. Then spend a little time thinking about the steps that you took to adapt to the situation. Use the following questions to get you started.

Have you ever been in physical danger?

Have you ever felt prejudged or misunderstood?

Have you ever felt a need to explain or justify your actions?

Have you ever sought to create a safe space or place for yourself?

Have you ever sought friendships with like-minded people and distanced yourself from other people?

Have you ever found yourself in a pecking order?

You might like to examine the ways in which you changed over time and so began to fit in situations where you had once felt yourself to be a stranger.

Commentary

What is true for each one of us is true for every child. Although the very young ones are still in the stages of building an identity, they are also preserving and protecting themselves. And, of course, kids in every classroom preserve and protect themselves every day. A student may look at a teacher as a potential ally or a potential enemy, and any word or action of the teacher will be filtered through that student's point of view. The practical impact is that a teacher may think that she is simply commenting about writing or science, but the student may feel that his self-esteem and safety are on the line.

Activity 2: Living Systems Can Be Influenced but Not Controlled

One of the most challenging aspects of education is the fact that we cannot know for certain how children will respond to various elements. This uncertainty is a consequence of some fundamental system properties.

Small Incidents Can Have Large Effects on a System

We have all had moments in our lives when a comment or incident changed everything. Sometimes a marriage or relationship changes. On occasion a friend's comment can lead to a flash of insight that lasts for years. A single momentary encounter with a friendly or unfriendly attendant can have an impact on our entire relationship with an organization.

Take some time to think about and discuss brief encounters, single incidents, or incidental comments that have had a major impact on your life.

Commentary

Small incidents pervade the classroom and the school. A child may see one chance encounter between a parent and a teacher that forever changes the child's attitude and expectations, irrespective of all the rules and lessons that may be covered in class about how people should interact. A teacher may not know a fact but pretend to know it, which pretense may forever color a student's attitude about truth and honesty, or about teachers.

This aspect of the ways in which people function means that our qualities as human beings are just as important to the people we teach as are our knowledge and our skill, and our everyday behaviors can have many far-reaching consequences. Professional development should require us to review ourselves as people with at least as much effort as we seek to improve our knowledge and skills.

Major Expenditures of Energy May Have No Result Whatsoever

We have all probably been party to at least one attempt to change things that has just not succeeded. It may be a neighborhood seeking to stop a development or to develop a community resource. It may be attempts to build a business, master a skill, or change a government policy. Similarly, most of us have probably been asked by a friend or loved one (perhaps quite strenuously over a long period of time) to change. And we simply have not.

Take some time to reflect on and discuss an experience in your life where a major investment of effort, time, and money got absolutely nowhere.

Commentary

Educators invest a lot of time, money, and effort to change instruction, curriculum, and student behavior. When we talk of fads that simply come and go, we are basically saying that the system absorbed all the energy, then went on as usual.

One fundamental characteristic of living systems is that they tend to have a very strong identity and can often just deflect or absorb efforts to change them. We see this characteristic in people who will not change—or learn— despite our best efforts. The key is to realize that the system is likely protecting itself, which means it must find its own internal reason to change.

➤ ### Activity 3: Every Living System Adapts to Its Entire Environment

Piaget spoke of assimilation and accommodation. *Assimilation* refers to the ability to simply absorb what is happening without changing. *Accommodation* means to adjust to what is happening and change if that is necessary for our survival and continued growth.

Adaptation is everywhere: in couples who change to preserve a good relationship, in animals that acquire new physical characteristics (such as species of birds that develop longer beaks over time to find food more efficiently), in professionals who take on the culture of their profession or place of business to succeed, in learners who encounter new information.

Take some time to recall and reflect on significant changes that you have made, both consciously and unconsciously, that have helped you to survive and succeed.

Commentary

Adaptation depends on our capacity to learn. We adapt to what we perceive to be real and important. Adaptation is constant, and much of it is unconscious. Moreover, we are simultaneously responding and adapting to what else is happening in the brain/mind as well as to the external environment, the "outside." Every person really is a complex system. And educators are always dealing with what someone once called the "squirming, active whole being of a child."

Challenge for Practice

We suffer from some enormous handicaps in traditional education. We act as though student behaviors can be fully separated from one another, as though they can be considered without regard to the whole student, and as though a student learns only one thing at a time. For instance, we tend to believe that the amount of time spent "on task" is the most important factor in learning. In fact, students learn from their entire experience, not just what we tell them is important.

Coming to terms with this complexity of the human brain, mind, and body can be very difficult. But no matter how we try to control or reduce learners to simple machines, until we appreciate just how complex they (and we ourselves) are, our ability to deal with the brain/mind will remain superficial.

A Question to Explore as a Learner

What do principle 1 and the ideas in this chapter suggest for your own learning?

Questions to Explore as an Educator

How is a lecture different from student participation in a large, real-life project?

Can lectures be living and lived experiences?

If so, under what circumstances?

Do you create groups in which students can work together?

In what circumstances is it better for students to work alone?

Do you ever discuss what happens to students during breaks and after school and relate it to the topic of the day?

To what extent do you respond to what is of immediate interest to students and relate it to the curriculum?

Do students have permission to go off on creative tangents at times?

Can you relate these tangents to the learning focus?

In what circumstances is it appropriate to insist on on-task behavior?

When you talk to students, do you expand their range of choices?

What could you do to create the same atmosphere in a classroom that students have when learning games outside of class?

And what is the difference between a meaningless and a meaningful game?

As you reflect on your discussions about the preceding questions, ask yourself these questions:

1. How does principle 1 challenge your assumptions about learning?

2. How does principle 1 challenge your assumptions about teaching?

3. How does principle 1 challenge your assumptions about discipline?

4. How does principle 1 challenge your assumptions about assessment?

Reality is both linear and nonlinear.

7

The Brain/Mind Is Social

Principle 2

David tells the story of standing on a street corner waiting to cross the street and looking down at his young son. He noticed, to his amazement, that his son was making the exact kinds of foot movements David tends to make when impatient. As he watched his son over a week, he saw other ways that his son was consciously and unconsciously imitating his own expressions and body movements.

One way in which we all become members who fit in a community is by socialization. Much of what we become is the result of imitation, as illustrated by David's son. Much is the result of reinforcement, as occurs when a baby says "mama" or "dada" or some variation that elicits delighted responses from adults and lots of encouragement to do it again. Much of what we become depends on those we adopt as our role models, frequently absorbing their characteristics and values peripherally and unconsciously, which is why we pay so much attention to the celebrities—actors, athletes, political leaders, and others—our children choose as role models.

> *It is through others that we master language, experience the magic of reading, learn to value other people and animals, model our behavior, see ourselves as lovable, capable, and intelligent, or not. Much of our self-image develops according to the feedback we get from others. The development of a self-image is driven further by biologically based drives to communicate, relate, and belong.*

Some Implications to Ponder

Note that the formation of social relationships depends on the type of community in which people find themselves, and community is under enormous pressure right now. One problem is the impact of television. Children in the United States see more than 20,000 commercials a year, and every year they watch television more hours than they spend in school. But television is a one-way medium that doesn't allow for challenging social interaction, especially with significant others, though it can wield significant influence. All people develop and test their theories about life, and without interactive opportunities in which to test what is promoted and suggested to them, children can grow up believing many "facts" that are unrelated to reality.

Information technology poses another challenge to traditional community. For instance, virtual communities featuring people who can remain anonymous are flourishing. This technology can also dramatically influence school life in ways such as the dissemination of information to people in various countries who are taking joint action to solve problems. Educators must come to terms with social dynamics and with the challenges posed and the promises offered by technology if they are to work with and capitalize upon the power of social relationship.

Building Interpersonal and Social Relationships

Social relationships and human interactions have an enormous impact on learning anything. In one sense educators have known about this impact because they have always been concerned with developing rules of civil inter-action in schools. However, social interaction is much more complex and intricate than educators have realized, and it influences everything that children learn—from math to science to art to belief in democracy and attitudes about other cultures. We invite you to begin your reflection on the topic by exploring the following questions.

Assume that we want children to learn to respect others. Which of the following approaches do you think is likely to have the greatest impact either individually or collectively? In what ways will each be effective or ineffective?

> **lessons from a teacher or principal on how to behave**

> **rewards and punishments administered arbitrarily for behavior that is not practiced by those administering the rewards and punishments**

> **a system that has some enforced protocols for living and working together**

a genuinely respectful and loving relationship experienced over time and modeled by adults in the environment

the behavior of teachers, nonteaching staff, and parents who naturally show respect toward one another when in front of children

the media and the signs of the dominant culture

For example, have you ever heard of the golfer Tiger Woods and his relationship with his father and mother? Are you aware of the impact that Tiger seems to have had on children and on the larger society? Describe the impact as you see it. What do you think was primarily responsible?

How might a child interpret all these facts about Tiger Woods? If you have never heard of Tiger Woods or about his familial relationships, how does it feel to be in a conversation where others take for granted something about which you know nothing?

➤ *Activity 1: Developing Social Relationships*

Observe, or spend a few moments remembering, children in
a school playground who are playing games or engaged in
other activities. You may like to think back over a period of
several days or weeks. Note any evidence of any of the
following:

competition for attention, dominance, or social status

cliques forming and being maintained

kids taking foolish risks to impress others

groups congregating in the same areas every day

lots of movement and shifting of positions

people not wanting to show that they are "smart" or "dumb"

the many different uses of language, from making friends to bossing other kids around

Note to what extent your observations show children imitating the language, postures, gestures, and behaviors of others: peers, parents, celebrities

Commentary

What you are observing are the hallmarks of complex societies in operation. Groups are bonding, people are being socialized, territory is being invaded and protected, egos are being challenged and defended, relationships are being formed, and so on. These activities are the subjects of disciplines as varied as sociology, psychology, history, anthropology, and biology. In other words, the basis for understanding how principle 2 works is also part of the foundation for many of the social sciences.

What is interesting is that such processes as bonding take place on the playground and in the classroom. Moreover, incidental learning takes place indirectly, even when students don't appear to be paying much attention.

➤ *Activity 2: Social Impacts on Learning*

- Imagine that you want a child to learn to read. The evidence is overwhelming that the best foundation for learning to read is to come from a home where there is a lot of reading. Why do you think this is the case?

- Many people have math phobia. Imagine that you want children to use math regularly and deeply understand that math is a part of life. Which environment is more likely to assist you in attaining this goal—one in which most teachers never use math openly except in lessons, or one in which math features naturally in teacher conversations and is used naturally in classrooms during math lessons and other times? Explore and discuss your thinking.

- Many children seem to take to computer games and computers easily and naturally. Most of them do so through exploring, investigating, and playing with others who are like-minded. What makes this method effective?

Commentary

The nature and quality of social interactions shape the nature of students' learning of content. We have all been forced to do something such as practice playing an instrument or memorize meaningless "stuff" only to avoid that very thing for the rest of our lives because the experience was so awful. The multiple facets of social relationship need to be as present in an educational environment as in any other environment. Just as the friendships among students help them to explore and appreciate the rules of a game, so friendships can help students grasp the function of grammar while they are putting together a newsletter. These social processes are involved in some ways in the construction of dynamical knowledge. We cannot stop them; we can only direct them.

In short, the quality of interaction, respect, caring, and authenticity (congruence between what we say and what we do) is a critical gateway to learners' accepting and using new information. Establishing and maintaining community are vital in brain-based learning.

Challenge to Practice

Students will search out social relationships. It is important that educators see this search as a natural and survival-oriented need, not a distraction. Classrooms and schools need to create positive, challenging, healthy learning environments that capitalize on social relationships. What we need to do as teachers is to integrate social learning with a challenging academic environment.

The problem is that children will "do as you do, not as you say." If we are sarcastic, students may learn that they are not respected. If we continually dominate in the classroom, we may teach helplessness or anger. If we love and know our subject, students may feel freer to ask complex questions and stretch their own learning.

A Question to Explore as a Learner

What do principle 2 and the ideas in this chapter suggest for your own learning?

Questions to Explore as an Educator

Many strategies directly and indirectly assist the building of healthy relationships: cooperative groups, research groups, peer teaching, democratic classrooms, authentic assessment that involves public displays and products, homework that requires interaction with adults. Which do you or might you use?

Might there be good and bad or appropriate and inappropriate ways to use such procedures as cooperative learning? How can we tell the difference?

To what extent will other aspects of the educational environment (such as assessment, age and grade divisions of students, class size, teacher expertise in content areas) influence attempts to build community and color social relationships?

Of course, adults also need good community if they are to create successfully such a community for children. We need to foster environments that support good listening and intellectual curiosity. Besides your process group, where else do you personally have the opportunity to learn and work in intellectually challenging, rich, social, and supportive situations?

As you reflect on your discussions about the preceding questions, ask yourself these questions:

1. **How does principle 2 challenge your assumptions about learning?**

2. **How does principle 2 challenge your assumptions about teaching?**

3. **How does principle 2 challenge your assumptions about discipline?**

4. **How does principle 2 challenge your assumptions about assessment?**

Inner and outer reflect each other.

8

The Search for Meaning Is Innate

We think it is Willis Harman who tells the story of two stone cutters who are carving blocks of stone. When asked what they are doing, the first replies, "I'm carving a block of stone." The second replies, "I'm building a cathedral." What counts, says Harman, is not what one is doing but what one is doing it for.

Our intrinsic motivation and need to know are two of our greatest gifts. The brain was designed as a meaning maker. We come into the world ready to explore and we learn through what we experience with our senses, guided by our need to know. The human brain is not passive. It doesn't wait to be fed; it aggressively goes after ever more knowledge from the time we are born.

It is possible for this drive to be undermined or for people to reach a comfort zone where they tend to stop searching for what is new but seek primarily to reinforce what they already believe. However, even when people are comfortable with their basic beliefs, *cognitive dissonance* (a conflict between what they believe and some other contradictory experience that they cannot doubt) forces them into a search for meaning. The development of aspects of modern physics such as quantum mechanics is riddled with examples of cognitive dissonance generated by experiments that were "impossible to believe," yet could not be doubted.

This principle reveals in more depth how the brain goes about actively organizing incoming information to make sense of life experience. The scientists such as Marie Curie, who spent hours, days, and years in a laboratory; the mathematicians such as Andrew Wiles, who spent seven years in relative seclusion in order to crack a mathematical puzzle called Fermat's last theorem; the artists such as Pablo Picasso, who rearranged and disturbed everyday patterns to communicate a sense of what he saw—these are people who illustrate the power of the search for meaning. And each one of us is born to function as both artist and scientist.

Maslow attempted to bring some order to all the things we need to know and the questions we ask by suggesting that we have a hierarchy of needs. Most fundamental are survival needs (food, water, shelter). Next are ego needs, then relationship needs. And finally is the ultimate need, which is to self-actualize, to become more fully human, to explore our unique capacities, and to understand what life itself is all about.

The bottom line is that learning and teaching must be related to the real questions that students ask, or must assist them to ask real questions. It is their purposes and questions, their hows and whys that provide a focus—a seed—around which meanings form. Those meanings will relate somehow to students' previous experiences, thoughts, and feelings. The brain/mind searches continually for these linkages. Indeed, the brain needs and automatically registers the familiar while simultaneously searching for and responding to novel stimuli. In effect, we are biologically programmed to make sense of our experience.

Experiment and Experience

The following activities will allow you to monitor some of the ways the brain/mind begins its search for meaning, the variety of feelings that accompany the brain's methods, and the variety of meanings that can be found in any given content.

➤ *Activity 1a: Observing Children*

Observe the ways in which young children explore their worlds. Watch them crawl, touch, move, taste, and seek attention.

What do you think they are trying to do?

In what ways are these actions a search for meaning?

Watch as adolescents imitate one another, model celebrities, adapt their dress and behavior to the expectations of peers, and engage in activities that are deeply absorbing.

What do you think they are trying to do?

In what ways are these actions a search for meaning?

Activity 1b: Observing Yourself in a New Place

Identify a setting in which you know you might feel a little strange and out of place. Examples include an industrial complex, an ethnic community, a cinema that features movies that you do not tend to see. Notice the ways in which you do each of the following:

look for landmarks and indicators that help you get a sense of where you are

react to dress and behavior codes that might be different from yours

compare where you are and what you see with people and places you find familiar

In what ways are these actions a search for meaning?

Commentary

Much of what drives people in a new context is the need to make sense of it. Indeed, much imitation and modeling of social behavior is also a search for meaning. The behaviors are driven by questions and questioning. This need causes people to engage in activities that range from developing spatial maps so they can navigate (as in finding our way out of a large airport) to identifying and evaluating behaviors that either comfort or threaten. All these activities are survival based.

All students try to establish context during their years in school. Sometimes they make instant judgments. The tendency to make such judgments is greater when they have downshifted (see principle 11) or are feeling relatively helpless to explore conclusions more deeply. But behind almost all behavior is a set of decisions people have made as to what makes sense for them. When people do not pay attention in class, for instance, they have usually decided that paying attention is essentially meaningless or not as meaningful as something else. Our job is to appreciate, then capitalize on and influence this never-ending search for meaning.

Activity 2: Reacting to Cultures Different from One's Own

Imagine that you are on a tour in a country other than your own and are told that you will be introduced to some aspects of Berkani life. You are informed that the Berkani view themselves as one with nature, and with natural rhythms and cycles. For them, even ordinary events are opportunities for celebration. The Berkani sing songs about planting corn and reenact the planting through dance. They view themselves as part of the planting process and as part of all natural occurrences. Explore and examine the sorts of meanings about life that would follow.

To what extent is your culture similar to and different from that of the Berkani?

Imagine that this connection to Earth appealed to you and that you suddenly realized that, by learning about cultures different from your own, you might learn how to make small events in your life more significant, your busy life less fragmented and more serene.

What new and different images and feelings would you have?

Commentary

The brain's/mind's search for meaning is very personal. The greater the extent to which what we learn is tied to personal, meaningful experiences, the greater and deeper our learning will be. As you ready yourself to understand the ways in which specific content can relate to your daily experience, note how the activity of your brain increases. You call to mind more images, perhaps feel greater anticipation, and picture specific situations in your life. In essence, the brain has already begun the ordering process of assimilating meaning.

As the brain/mind processes experience, it always searches for connections. The extent to which we are transformed by our experiences is the extent to which they are meaningful to us. This activity requires us to assimilate meaning at a number of levels. We will each come away with our own kind of knowledge, depending on the impact of the information, example, and our experiences.

For instance, some may well have thought that celebrating an ordinary event for a week was useless or ridiculous. They may have made no connections with formalized celebrations such as holidays. Others might begin to feel that all of life can be viewed as an ongoing celebration. Yet others may have discovered a different way of experiencing the ordinary events of life.

Activity 3: Reintroduction to the Arts

Einstein was a musician. Churchill was a painter. And da Vinci was a scientist. Each had, among other things, a very vivid and powerful imagination. Each asked potent questions. Take some time to ponder the relationship between success in arts and some other field.

If it is true that some of our understanding can be communicated only nonverbally or in verbal forms where feeling and imagery prevail, then do we deprive people of the opportunity to understand and communicate when we exclude the arts from their everyday lives?

To what extent might exposure to the practice of art help students naturally gain an appreciation for high standards?

To what extent do you think their artistic explorations and proficiency assisted Einstein, Churchill, and da Vinci to master other domains? What sorts of questions do you think the three people were really asking?

Commentary

It is important to realize that the arts are not all alike and do not function in identical ways. However, they represent, among other things, ways of exercising imagination and of giving expression to meanings and powerful ideas. Increasing evidence shows that the arts have a powerful, peripheral impact on people. At least as important as anything else is the capacity of art to be a vehicle for asking questions that are at the heart of the search for meaning.

Challenge to Practice

The need to make sense of the world doesn't go away when children enter school. But what appears to happen is that we move away from their questions to our agenda. We no longer organize their learning around their purposes or meanings. As a matter of fact, much of their learning is rote or relatively meaningless. We are not saying that memorization is wrong in all contexts, only when it is devoid of social or personal meaning and purpose. When memorization is overemphasized, students begin to separate learning in the real world from school learning and reserve their genuine questions for the world outside school.

Connecting students to their own meanings and tying these meanings to a purpose is a central consideration in brain-compatible teaching. Most of us are so used to structuring learning around our adult and professional purposes, such as district mandates, unit plans, and daily lesson plans, that giving students an opportunity to learn based on their own search for meaning (their genuine questions) seems almost impossible. Yet forcing students to learn things they don't care about is fundamentally less effective; it is actually harder for the brain/mind to process information it finds meaningless.

The brain/mind naturally searches for meaning in experience, and every moment of students' class and school life is an experience that they interpret. For students to master content appropriately, we must teach content for meaningful connections to students' lives.

Two essential ingredients of brain-compatible learning apply here. One is to immerse the learner in multiple, complex interactive experiences, what we call *orchestrated immersion.* The other is active processing, the "consolidation and internalization of information, by the learner, in a way that is both personally meaningful and conceptually coherent" (Caine and Caine 1994, 147). In other words, we take advantage of learners' innate drive to make sense by creating appropriate experiences and then helping them process those experiences in multiple ways. We can facilitate, and to some extent give direction to, the generation of a student's natural knowledge.

A Question to Explore as a Learner

What do principle 3 and the ideas in this chapter suggest for your own learning?

Questions to Explore as an Educator

How do you get to meaningful learning and students' genuine questions?

How do you embed in experience the facts and skills that students need to master?

What changes would such embedding mean for us as educators?

How do you know what real questions students have? In how many ways do you provide opportunities for them to express their questions?

In what ways do you provide examples and ask questions that relate specifically to the experience of students whenever you teach?

In what ways do you create experiences, activities, or simulations from which students can process content and skills?

In what ways do you genuinely engage the imagination of students?

In what ways do you provide opportunities for students to share their own meanings and interpretations? What more could you do?

In what ways do you encourage students to build bridges between what they learn and what they already know?

As you reflect on your discussions about the preceding questions, ask yourself these questions:

1. **How does principle 3 challenge your assumptions about learning?**

2. **How does principle 3 challenge your assumptions about teaching?**

3. **How does principle 3 challenge your assumptions about discipline?**

4. **How does principle 3 challenge your assumptions about assessment?**

Order is present everywhere.

9

The Search for Meaning Occurs through Patterning

Jimmy is growing his first garden. He digs up a bit of the backyard, and he makes rows with the toe of his shoe. Then he opens a little packet of beans that his mother bought him and plants them all in the same row. Next he covers up all the rows, then gets a hose and soaks the entire bed until it is overflowing. Then he runs off to play somewhere else. He forgets the garden for the next few days, but when his mother reminds him that plants need water, he rushes off to get the hose, turns it on as powerfully as he can, and blasts all the rows unmercifully. Then he turns the hose off and goes back to inspect the garden. Seeing no plants of any kind, he calls out, "Mummy, Mummy, when will my beans grow?"

Jimmy understands some facts and has developed some patterns regarding plants, but they are incomplete. For instance, he knows that seeds need to be put in soil and watered. But he does not know how or when to water, nor about the impact of water pressure, nor how long it takes for plants to grow. His ideas and beliefs need to be challenged and expanded. As his knowledge and understanding grow, he will develop operating schema and will have much more success with his plants. In effect, he needs to master patterns that work. In terms of the brain, he is developing specialized neural circuits.

A pattern is what Fritjof Capra (1998) calls "a configuration of relationships" (80), in other words, a set or combination of things that seem to fit together. Whenever we try to figure out what something means, we search for patterns that make sense to us. As we say in chapter 3, "At the heart of patterning is categorization—finding similarities and differences and comparing and isolating features. We are all born with the ability to interpret the world around us by sorting its countless characteristics into categories. For example, we observe and sort lines, edges, and curves; light and dark, up and down, basic smells and tastes, and degrees of sound. Our brains are even prewired with a basic number sense that gives very young infants a rudimentary awareness of the relationship among the numbers one through three. With experience, these abilities combine and gel into more complex categories such as 'trees' and 'people.' Over time, richer and richer clusters of patterns take shape in our minds."

These patterns become the lenses through which we look at and come to understand our experience. Sometimes they are invented and literally have to be taught, such as with phonemes, sounds that comprise the letters of the alphabet and the core components of words. The capacity to find and create patterns is the indispensable heart of learning. The brain/mind has many ways to create patterns, and we touch on a few of them in this work.

One way to look at any subject in the curriculum is as a set of new patterns that we want students to develop so that they are better equipped to understand their lives. The problem is that patterning occurs naturally, inside the brain/mind of the learner. We cannot force people to see a pattern, though we can help them see it. The educational philosophy of constructivism states that educators must assist students in developing their own grasp of the patterns inherent in each subject.

We three can describe the patterning process by repeating that we each can look at the world as both scientist and artist. As scientists, we observe and seek to explain or understand what we experience. As artists, we continually create and generate patterns that express what we think and feel.

Exploring Patterning

Look at some of the basic aspects of patterning that are particularly important to education.

➤ ### *Activity 1: Predisposition to Connect Things That Seem to Be Related in Space and Time*

Perceptual psychology shows that we all have some basic capacities and predispositions to perceive patterns. For instance, we tend to group things that are close together. And we tend to fill in the gaps and make assumptions when information is missing. For example, we might make an assumption about what a man or woman alone on a street at night might be up to.

Observing Things That Seem to Fit Together

Take a walk down any street and look for items that seem to be naturally connected.

Is there a difference in the ways that leaves seem to be connected to one another on a tree and when they are lying on the ground?

What is the difference between your perception of plants in garden beds and plants in fields or alongside a sidewalk?

Compare a single shop to a cluster of shops and stores that you see in a mall. What is the difference between a group of people who are wandering in the streets and the crowd flowing out of a football stadium after the game?

Intentionally Making Things Fit Together

Learn the following abstract symbols as quickly as you can. As you do so, note the process through which you learn the symbols.

A = ⌐	D = ⌐	G = ⌐
B = ⌐	E = □	H = ⌐
C = ⌐	F = ⌐	I = ⌐

Now examine the diagram on page 107; note the ease with which you can now grasp and recall the same symbols.

Commentary

The basic implication is that instruction and the curriculum should be designed so things fit together naturally for students. One key step is to provide students with enough information. But information is not just more facts. It includes extensive, supporting sensory input in a relevant and coherent context, one of the essential foundations for the development of language, for instance. The organizing power of the rich context is also why children who come from an environment rich in reading materials usually learn to read more quickly and easily than those from an environment lacking such materials—and why one key to teaching reading is to create literature-rich environments rich in literature in school.

A	B	C
D	E	F
G	H	I

➤ **Activity 2: Concepts**

Concepts are essentially organizing ideas; they make facts meaningful. Once a concept is really grasped, facts can be remembered much more easily. We all rely on concepts for much of our patterning, even though many people are hard put to define *concept* when asked to do so. Of course, people may have fundamentally different concepts, even if they use the same words to describe them. And in cases where they do not have a concept, we freely say, "They just don't get it."

Let's explore the difference between facts and concepts by using two examples, *forest* and *democracy*. It is easy to be told and to remember that a forest is a collection of trees. However, a person who grasps the idea of a forest is much more able to recognize one, talk about one, and even live in one. We can also attempt to define democracy and ask students to remember the definition and examples of democracies. But it takes people who genuinely appreciate what a democracy is all about to engage willingly in discussion on controversial issues, give those with opinions different from theirs an opportunity to express those opinions, participate in voting, and support the outcomes, even when working to change the outcome the next time. Concepts create relationships between facts. They are critical to understanding.

Compare some aspect of your life where you have grasped the concept with one where you haven't; perhaps you could compare using a computer to gardening.

How would you characterize the differences?

Is one easier to learn about than another? Why and in what ways?

How do the differences feel?

Commentary

Right at the heart of meaningful learning is the capacity to get the concepts rather than just list the facts. And right at the heart of effective living is the ability to grasp the concepts on which services, social organization, and the world of nature are based. What is democracy? Why are government and business different, and how are they similar? What is the point of recycling? Why do trees and plants need water regularly? What is it about conflict resolution that makes relationships easier? How does saving a little bit every month add up to a large amount over time? A critical point is that the core patterns that make life work depend on organizing ideas—concepts—and these are different from facts and memorized procedures.

➤ *Activity 3: Metaphor*

New discoveries and insights in various fields and subjects often tend to be conveyed by the use of metaphor or by the expanded use of familiar concepts. Examples include black holes in physics, the periodic table and chemical bonding in chemistry, and the water cycle in the earth sciences.

Spend some time searching any subject you teach or in which you are interested for the core metaphors that you use to explain central concepts.

From where do those metaphors come?

What aspects of the metaphor are most useful in conveying core ideas?

Do the metaphors miscommunicate in any way?

In general, how useful and important are they?

Commentary

New ideas are essentially new patterns that learners need to perceive. A practical tool for teaching new patterns is to work with the learner to identify, then to explore and unpack crucial metaphors. Sometimes the arts are the best process through which to examine metaphors.

Five patterns that occur frequently in nature are listed below:

- Hexagons
- Branches
- Meanderings
- Spirals
- Explosions

You will see patterns repeated in many ways in the illustrations in this book. Take some time to look for them in your environment. Note that these patterns are also metaphorical. The plot of a story may branch out, a character in a novel can explode with passion. Learning and teaching about almost anything, in fact, are enhanced by the use and power of metaphor.

Challenge for Practice

The essence of meaningful learning is the students' perception and generation of patterns that are useful and make sense to them. Our task as educators is to introduce into all that we do the opportunity for students to engage in richer patterning: to grasp the concepts, themes, categories, and metaphors. Thus we need to build opportunities and design experiences around preselected patterns.

You will see that experience itself has an organizing power. In fact, it is likely to force you to rearrange the way in which you might otherwise have developed the material you are teaching. Part of our job is to embed material in experiences so that meaningful patterns can emerge. We elaborate on this embedding process in part 3 of this book.

We also need to create the sense of freedom and an atmosphere that encourages students to search for and create unique patterns. Using art and music, and asking students to learn about art and music, are practical ways to accomplish this sense of freedom. We can begin by keeping in mind questions that guide us in ways of thinking about patterns and about curriculum and instruction.

A Question to Explore as a Learner

What do principle 4 and the ideas in this chapter suggest for your own learning?

Questions to Explore as an Educator

Review what we mean by *patterning*.

What kinds of patterns do you teach?

What do you think is the difference between a complex and a simple pattern?

In what ways do you create a learning context in which the search for patterns is an ongoing challenge and expectation?

In what ways do you seek and convey threads or themes that may be inherent in various subjects you teach?

In what ways do you use an interdisciplinary approach in teaching at times so that you go beyond the boundaries of single subjects?

In what ways do you ask students about the related personal experiences that the learning of particular content evokes in them?

In what ways do you create an environment in which students may discover patterns and meanings for themselves or through interaction with others rather than telling them what the patterns are?

Select one aspect of your curriculum. Look for ways in which the elements that you are teaching can be fully embedded in some real-life experience of your students.

As you reflect on your discussions about the preceding questions, ask yourself these questions:

1. **How does principle 4 challenge your assumptions about learning?**

2. **How does principle 4 challenge your assumptions about teaching?**

3. **How does principle 4 challenge your assumptions about discipline?**

4. **How does principle 4 challenge your assumptions about assessment?**

Reality consists of matter, energy, and meaning.

10

Emotions Are Critical to Patterning

Principle 5

The stars are still shining in the sky as I crawl out of my tent. In a short time I will resume my excavations of the ancient city. I feel the morning in the glimmer of the fading moon. My hands rub together almost instinctively, trying to generate some warmth. I am awestruck by the thought that the Sun is millions of degrees K while the ambient temperature where I am is almost zero. I reflect on recent discoveries concerning the dramatic climatic changes across the face of Earth in the last 40,000 years. And I ponder the ways in which people of ancient times, particularly during the Ice Ages, kept warm with almost no technology of the sort that I take for granted.

Why do mornings like this always seem out of the ordinary? Building a fire, I wait impatiently for my first cup of coffee. Finally I hear the gurgling noise that signals the end of a short eternity. What did happen during the Ice Ages? I ask myself. Amid the quiet morning sounds I pour my first cup. I sit back, look at the waking world around me, warm my hands almost sensuously around the cup, and drink my first taste. The morning is perfect.

We need to go far beyond the traditional view that our task is simply to help students feel supported and safe. We must grasp the profound interaction of cognition and emotion. There are at least two ways in which cognition and emotion interact.

1. In part, it is our emotions that tell us how significant or insignificant something is, and what value to place on it. And everything that we ultimately learn, without exception, is valued or devalued in some way. That is, we either want to, or don't want to, keep learning or use what we learned. It becomes clear that *intrinsic motivation* describes a personal emotional attachment that a person has to a project or activity, and that emotional energy is part of what keeps the person going. The more we assist students to tap into their intrinsic motivation, the less we need to worry about "discipline" or "time on task."

2. The meaning of any idea, concept, or skill is partly determined by how we feel about it and how we relate to it. This implication is far more radical than the first because it suggests that, to understand anything fully, a person needs to relate to it emotionally. Because education has focused so much on requiring the storing of information and facts, the second idea seems counterintuitive. However, it is now clear that real knowledge, which involves knowing something so well that we can use it to explain and navigate in our world, has an emotional component.

As educators we cannot force students to connect with some idea or subject (such as math). All we can do is create conditions that contribute to either their relating to and appreciating a subject or hating it. That sense of relationship is characteristic of the relationship that experts have with their fields of expertise. We must work with that "feel" from the very beginning. That is why Gendlin's (1981) notion of "felt meaning," which we define as an unarticulated sense of relationship that culminates in the "aha" of insight, is so pertinent here.

The key is to grasp this relationship between emotion, understanding, and meaning, then to learn how to create the conditions that contribute to felt meaning.

Exploring Feeling and Emotion

The brain is patterning all the time, and those patterns of understanding are intrinsically emotional. Emotional "color" is actually part of meaning. Explore this aspect of learning in several ways.

 ### *Activity 1: Feelings about Experiences*

Recall some of the following occasions and note your feelings and emotions as you recount the details of each.

a holiday, perhaps in your youth, when there was laughter, warmth, and love

a sad occasion that left you overwrought

a time when you felt victorious

a special romantic occasion

Commentary

Emotions influence the intensity and vividness of our memories. Emotions also shape and color our memories. Physical reactions also accompany memories heavy with emotion. There may be smiles, frowns, tears, tension, increased pulse rate, and hormonal changes. As we saw in the discussion of the first two principles, our bodies react physically and emotionally to experience and to thoughts about experience.

 ## Activity 2: Feelings about Words and Concepts

Look at the following list one word at a time and note the feelings each evokes. Sometimes it helps for one person to read the list slowly while the others listen.

house   bird   learning

police   pet

school   flower

flag   hospital   test

democracy   friend

Commentary

If you pay close attention you'll be able to catch a feeling and an attitude you have about each word, but even registering no response is significant. Chances are your feelings are different from someone else's because of your past experiences and associations.

Activity 3: Feelings about Subjects and Skills

Repeat activity 2 using subjects and skills you might have studied. Following are some examples to get you started:

art   biology
                    math
literature   history
                    computing

Commentary

At a very basic level, our attitudes about what we studied are highly emotional. Indeed, we can be programmed or conditioned into disliking what we have to study or learn. We might learn to draw but dislike drawing, while we struggle through adversity to master math because we find the process exciting. Our challenge as educators is to enliven our subjects so students have positive emotional attitudes toward education generally and to individual subjects specifically.

 ## Activity 4: Emotional Responses to Events

For one complete day, record in your journal your emotional responses to various events (such as the news) and messages (such as administrative requirements). Explore the extent to which your understanding of the event or message depends on, is inhibited by, or is shaped by your emotional response.

Commentary

This activity illustrates the multiple ways in which emotions permeate our lives. It is as though we are in an emotional bath.

Activity 5: Emotional Aspects of Metaphor

Read each phrase that follows. Note the emotion or situation you believe is expressed in each phrase. Then state the literal meaning of the phrase.

He is burning with desire.

She is an angel.

I was hopping mad.

She is sponging off them.

They are blowing off steam.

She is the apple of his eye.

Commentary

These sentences use metaphors to create images from which we extract certain meanings. Lakoff and Johnson (1980) give many examples of this metaphorical use of language. For instance, we think of time as a commodity—we "budget" time, "save" it, "run out of" it, "manage" it, "lose" it, or "waste" it. We see arguments often in terms of war: we "win" arguments, "lose" them, "defend" positions.

Metaphors do more than make our language more colorful. They add feeling and enrich meaning. They also help us add to patterning, whether we are looking at words, schema, codes, assumptions, or emotions. Metaphors are deeply linked to patterns that reflect our construction of meanings and reality.

➤ Activity 6: Feelings and Opinions

Note and discuss some opinions that you have held for many years. Reflect on how strongly you hold them. Ask yourself, "What sort of evidence and experience would it take for me to change my mind?" Some examples follow:

political beliefs

opinions about practices in cultures different from your own

your ability to excel at playing a particular sport, playing a musical instrument, making financial investments, managing your time, learning another language, doing math, having healthy relationships, or some other area

Commentary

We see that our assumptions about how things are or should be are anchored in our feelings and emotions. The emotion with which individual people react to an action or suggestion is a key to what they really think, even when to the best of their knowledge they think something else. Our mental models involve beliefs and assumptions that are grounded in feelings and emotions.

As we develop our worldviews, contoured and colored by emotions, values, and expectations, we naturally interpret new experiences in terms of patterns that we have already established. Students face a new year of math with the mindset they acquired earlier. Bigotry and prejudice are extreme examples of closed patterns. Ellen Langer (1989) calls these fixed patterns *category traps*. We all have them, and they act as barriers to new learning.

Challenge to Practice

When we see teaching as no more than getting information into a student, we miss the richness with which the human brain deals with reality and overlook the much broader spectrum of information that is "there." A fundamental and devastatingly counterproductive consequence of teaching this way is that students seem to "master" a subject by doing well on tests, yet be demotivated from pursuing that subject and largely unaware of what a subject is really all about.

Helping people acquire a feeling for a subject is very different from merely explaining it to them. Building a sense of relationship with a subject, idea, or skill is a little bit like developing a friendship with someone. Occasionally we find a perfect, immediate match. But usually it takes time to get to know each other. In developing friendships, we need multiple encounters, we explore purposes and beliefs, and we discuss interests. There may be ups and downs, agreements and misunderstandings, acceptance and forgiveness. Ultimately, friendship happens. Learning anything in depth involves many of the same ups and downs to make connections.

A Question to Explore as a Learner

What do principle 5 and the ideas in this chapter suggest for your own learning?

Questions for You as Educator

How might you teach or administer an educational environment if your goal were to help students connect with or relate to a subject as one crucial aspect of coming to understand it?

In what ways do you or can you create an environment that genuinely values what students think?

How would you really know how a student feels about a subject or project?

Is it possible to enjoy and relate to a subject or skill that is really difficult to master? Where does the joy come from?

In what ways do you act as though students should feel the same way you do? In what ways do you or can you give them freedom to discover their own feelings?

In what ways do you or can you balance honoring the way students feel with challenging them to think and feel differently?

As you reflect on your discussions about the preceding questions, ask yourself these questions:

1. **How does principle 5 challenge your assumptions about learning?**

2. **How does principle 5 challenge your assumptions about teaching?**

3. **How does principle 5 challenge your assumptions about discipline?**

4. **How does principle 5 challenge your assumptions about assessment?**

Everything is both part and whole simultaneously.

11

Every Brain Simultaneously Perceives and Creates Parts and Wholes

To see a world in a grain of sand,
And a Heaven in a wild flower,
Hold Infinity in the palm of your hand,
And Eternity in an hour.

—William Blake
Songs of Innocence

Imagine you are looking at a painting. The image may be a scene in nature or a city, or even a basket of fruit. Notice how your brain takes in the entire picture but also stays aware of very specific details. You identify brush strokes, colors that constitute changes in light or intensity. The human brain is capable of visualizing the whole and managing the fine details, highly specific skills, and knowledge contained in that whole.

There is a perfect match between the brain/mind and the world in which it finds itself; that is, we all have many natural capacities for simultaneously being aware of some of the parts and wholes of experience.

As we mention in chapter 3, for instance, the two hemispheres of the neocortex each have some different functions, yet are designed to work together. A great deal of additional evidence supports the theory of overlapping functions and the interrelationship of parts and wholes. An example of the former is that some training in music assists people to develop spatial intelligence. An example of the latter is that regions of the brain that regulate specific functions (such as the role of the amygdala with emotions and the hippocampus with memory) are intricately connected.

In education, we largely ignore this principle. Either we focus heavily on isolated facts and skills to be mastered, or we create "global" experiences such as field trips or social events but fail to explore specific issues, embed specific skills in these experiences, or pay attention to emotional reactions. Our collective educational challenge is to design the curriculum to capitalize on these natural brain/mind capacities to integrate parts and wholes.

The process of integrating content and life experience is quite complex, and teachers need to be relatively expert in the subjects they teach. In fact, they must realize that every subject deeply interpenetrates every other subject. We can use history as an example. Any point in history comes as a result of what passed before it and shapes the future, which is now our present. Learning history is never simply a matter of memorizing specific events, dates, and places. History consists of living, thinking, breathing, and feeling people who created a reality. The poetry that people of individual cultures compose is forged by their experiences. Their literature reflects their hopes, dreams, disappointments, and physical realities. Their music and songs reflect the joys and pains of human life on Earth. Their technology, agriculture, economics, and art are connected in experience.

A Sense of the Whole

Arthur Koestler coined the term *holon* to describe the condition in which everything is a part of something larger and a whole of which other things are a part.

➤ ## *Activity 1: Exploring Holons*

This exercise is designed to clarify how intimately everything is connected to some greater reality, that larger realities contain parts, and that nothing really exists or stands alone. It is also designed to demonstrate that the brain is capable of holding a range of images at once and that teaching needs to respect the parts and the larger context in which the parts participate.

Step 1: Play some relaxing music that induces a reflective state—perhaps some great classical music or a tape specifically designed to provide relaxing background sound. Lean back and take a few deep breaths.

Step 2: Once you feel relaxed, read the italicized passage that follows to yourself or have someone read it slowly to you. Experiment and learn from your reactions so that you understand better how to use this method in your teaching. In the text, each ellipsis should take approximately three seconds. The less experience you or your group has with using imagery, however, the longer the pauses at the ellipses should be. As you read, engage as many of your senses, as much of your intellect and emotion as possible. The richer the experience, the more potential there is to expand your awareness at deep levels.

Look at one of your hands . . . Imagine that you are inside a zoom lens moving ever closer to your hand . . . You are now inside the skin . . . now inside the cells . . . When you are ready, move to the atoms that make up your hand . . . then to subatomic levels . . .

Slowly move back up from the subatomic level . . . to the atoms that make up your hand . . . to skin and hand . . . Now step back a bit and see your hand as part of your arm . . . your body . . . the room you are in . . . the house . . .

Zoom out to include the neighborhood . . . your state . . . the country . . . the planet . . . the solar system . . . and the galaxy . . . Now come back step by step to the point where you began . . .

Step 3: Answer the following questions:

How does the interconnectedness feel?

Did you feel it in any specific part of your body? Do you now?

What emotions (positive, negative, or neutral) did you experience?

Would you do the exercise again? What would you change if you did?

What would you watch for if you were to lead someone else through this exercise?

Which part of the sequence can you eliminate and still experience your hand in this moment? The cells? The atoms? Your body? The house? Perhaps move outdoors in your mind. Would this hand exist without a planet? A solar system? A universe?

What does *interconnectedness* mean to you? Of what does it remind you? How would you define it? Where do you find it in life?

Is anything not part of the greater whole?

Commentary

Most education focuses on each facet of learning as a
discrete object of study, not as an event that touches and
defines others. However, every experience contains the
continuum you just experienced with the journey in and
beyond your hand. Every curricular segment we focus on
is somehow related and connected to other elements and
events. Understanding these connections is not only crucial
to learning differently, it is at the heart of the thinking that
helps you change the way you teach.

Natural Wholes

There are many ways to organize information and experience
so that the natural whole becomes evident. The arts,
stories, and projects are all powerful tools for education at
every level, from prekindergarten to post-graduate.

Stories

We naturally perceive and relate to stories. Children acquire
a sense of narrative when they are very young. And early
humans developed stories to pass on religious, historical,
scientific, and cultural knowledge. Subsequent generations
added new versions and developed extensive ways to
express the meaning these stories communicated. During
nostalgic times we often recount moments of the saga of our
selves. Almost every detailed item in the news is in story
form. The power of and fascination with stories continue
through our entire lives.

In part the power of story is a consequence of a particular
memory system—the locale memory system dealt with in
more depth in chapter 14. That memory system is largely
autobiographical and registers our own life stories.

Activity 2: Exploring Stories

Explore some of the ways in which stories infuse your life.

Discuss the extent to which items in the news are framed as stories, for example, a reporter is introduced with the phrase "X has the story on that."

With your group, share your knowledge on ways in which people in earlier times passed on their knowledge, customs, and beliefs by means of stories.

With your group, share your knowledge about the basic elements of a story (plot, characters) and the types of stories there are (historical, narrative).

How much of your daily conversations with others are in the form of stories of some type? Discuss daily conversations with your group.

Commentary

There is a sense of wholeness, connectedness, and meaning that is conveyed in a story that would otherwise be only irrelevant fragments of experience. A majority of our personal communication is telling stories of particular incidents in our day-to-day lives.

Students' engagement increases noticeably when a teacher tells a story rather than merely presenting facts. When a story illustrates a larger truth that can be examined through subsequent activity, it takes on even greater power.

 ### Activity 3: Projects

A project has a purpose that naturally organizes people's attention and efforts. Setting up a business, designing the layout for a brochure, installing a computer network, designing and maintaining a garden, creating a new flower-bed—these are all projects. And they are all wholes of which there are parts.

Examine some projects in which you have been engaged recently.

How did they organize your time?

What sorts of questions did they invoke?

Commentary

A project tends to begin with a sense of the whole even as we consider the many specific elements that we need to work out. For the most part projects have purposes, beginnings, and endings, and they take place in relatively well defined places. Many include the opportunity to form relationships with others. And projects do not come into existence out of nowhere. They grow out of something larger. Sometimes they are part of the ongoing life story and career of an individual. Sometimes they are part of a larger project such as setting up a business. And these larger things are also part of something larger still. Hence, as with stories, there is a natural sense of wholeness and connectedness.

Activity 4: Parts and Wholes in Art and Science

Why the Arts Are Important to Science

There are many reasons for the connection between art and science, including the need to be very good observers, to persevere, and to work with intuition. These capacities involve integrating what split-brain research initially identified as different properties of the two hemispheres of the neocortex—the analytical and the intuitive (see chapter 3).

As an exercise, select a great artist and a great scientist. Study some of their work and look for some of the ways in which they needed to master and integrate parts and wholes. An impressionist painter, for example, might use a lot of bits of color to create an overall scene; a biologist might examine many different species to understand an ecosystem.

Scientists have long said that the best of their breed are artistically inclined. Most everyone has seen photos of Einstein with his violin and physicist Richard Feynman with his bongos . . . Nobel Prize-winning chemist Roald Hoffmann writes highly praised poetry (only sometimes about molecules).

Put four mathematicians in a room, the old saying goes, and you are sure to have a string quartet.

In fact, artistically inclined scientists tend to win more awards than their less diversified colleagues, according to several studies.

—K. C. Cole

Commentary

Art and science interact in multiple ways. Each illustrates that brain/mind functioning is complex, and they reinforce the need to teach that allows for the parts and wholes to interact continuously. Each can be used to help students grasp and master the other, so that fine arts and science teachers can be natural partners. And each can reveal how an awareness of the relationship of parts to whole is crucial to the pattern detection discussed in chapter 9. To continue Cole's quotation: "Painting, piano playing, and poetry help put things in context, sharpen details, hone observations. They sort the essential from the peripheral, forge connections, find patterns, and discover new ways of seeing familiar things. These are exactly the tools any good scientist needs" (B1).

Challenge to Practice

A fundamental challenge for educators is to appreciate and work with the ways in which parts are embedded in wholes. The whole is the organizer; the parts are what fill in the whole. Both contribute to meaning, and we lose meaning when we ignore, discount, or misunderstand either.

Much of the thrust of the brain/mind learning principles is that many elements go into the making of a whole. We want you to grasp the nature of wholeness and some of the natural wholes that the brain/mind uses. Your immediate task, we suggest, is to see how these natural wholes fit into the curriculum and the classroom.

It is not uncommon, for instance, for a geometry teacher to teach about rectangles, squares, parallel lines, and circles without ever referring to how these geometric figures play themselves out in the natural world and the world outside the classroom. But projects such as designing the sprinkler system for a school can integrate these notions wonderfully.

A Question to Explore as a Learner

What do principle 6 and the ideas in this chapter suggest for your own learning?

Questions to Explore as an Educator

In your work, how do you and can you incorporate the following?

stories

projects

simulations

the arts

integration of the curriculum

thematic instruction

ecological thinking

How much time and what sort of organization does it take to incorporate these elements effectively?

Is there ever a difference between your view of the parts and a whole and the students' views of parts and a whole? What does that difference mean for your practice?

Do you regard the various processes listed in the first question as separate or connected? In what ways might they be connected?

Every chapter in this book that deals with a brain/mind learning principle is preceded by a photograph and what we call a *principle of connectedness*. How do the photographs and accompanying principles contribute to your understanding of the nature of wholeness?

As you reflect on your discussions about the preceding questions, ask yourself these questions:

1. **How does principle 6 challenge your assumptions about learning?**

2. **How does principle 6 challenge your assumptions about teaching?**

3. **How does principle 6 challenge your assumptions about discipline?**

4. **How does principle 6 challenge your assumptions about assessment?**

Everything comes in layers.

12

Learning Involves Both Focused Attention and Peripheral Perception

A family goes out for the day. They travel for a while and decide to take time out for a meal. They head into a fast-food hamburger place, which is decorated in bright vivid colors. They eat their meal and pull out in short order. As they leave, they glance at a newspaper headline and find themselves engaged in a fierce conversation about politics as the trip continues. Suddenly one of them sees a sign to a lakeside recreation area. They all agree to explore and pull off the freeway. They find themselves on a country road, with green fields and lush trees all around. They slow the car to a more leisurely pace. They pull up at a deep blue lake and, to their surprise, find no one else there. The children go off for a swim, and the parents unconsciously take a deep breath of relief as they settle down to enjoy the surroundings. A gentle breeze, shaded blanket of lawn, and the utter quiet remove almost all traces of the outside world. A few hours later, with children chattering happily, they pile back into their car and head for home. Back on the freeway, notwithstanding their delightful interlude, they pick up speed and travel bumper to bumper with other traffic,

swerving to avoid lane changers and accelerating to escape from tail-gating trucks, losing much of the repose they had acquired. Fortunately they arrive home without incident.

The family has been functioning on at least two levels. On one level, they have been acting with purpose, paying attention to specific aspects of their trip—the place to eat, the place to play, the drive home. But at the same time, on a different level, they have been heavily influenced, both directly and indirectly, by aspects of their surroundings.

The fast-food restaurant sign was painted in colors selected to attract them and to stimulate their appetite. The colors and the overall design were intended to get them in—and to get them out quickly! The newspaper headline was designed and positioned as an attention getter—and it worked. Once in the country, the slower pace, the serenity of the environment, the colors, and the absence of hustle and bustle all contributed to their becoming more relaxed— again largely without their being aware of the surroundings. When they got back on the freeway, they got caught up in the vigor, speed, and flow of the traffic; they were entrained by it so that they began to drive just like other drivers without being aware of the fact. Every one of these environments has affected the state of their physiology and brain.

The dance we observe is between general perception of the environment and selective attention to various aspects of it. We all move through life engaged in this ongoing dance. We are all powerfully influenced by signals and stimuli from the environment that we perceive and that color and create a context for whatever we actually choose to focus on. Advertisers, for example, position their advertisements in the context of programs that stimulate identifiable desires and fears in selected audiences. Diane Halpern (1989) tells of a conversation she once had with a cab driver. She and the driver had been discussing the way in which laundry products are advertised on television. The cab driver insisted that he never paid any attention to such advertising and that he always just got the blue bottle that got out "ring around the collar." Halpern goes on to say, "Although he believed that he was not allowing the advertising claims to influence him, in fact, they were directly determining his buying habits" (8) as evidenced by his repeating the slogan.

> *The interplay between perception and attention has immense importance for education. It is critical that students pay attention and focus on a single question for extended periods of time. At the same time, students in a school are profoundly influenced by the total environment.*

Attention and Perception

In this section we examine a few aspects of attention and perception, beginning with sensory input and the way in which it is organized.

 ## *Activity 1: Sensory Input*

Find a scene or bring to mind a scene such as a mall or a lake. It is worth your time to actually observe some real event or scenario rather than visualizing it, but if you must visualize, do so as vividly as possible.

Notice the direct sensory input—the colors, the lighting, the motion, the rustle of wind, the roar of traffic, and so on. Notice how all your senses respond.

Next, itemize the various objects and activities that you see: trees, people, houses, cars moving down roads, signs, and so on.

Commentary

The first goal of this activity is for you to become more aware of the sensory foundation we experience. The second goal is to show that we all automatically organize this sensory input into categories, maps, and patterns we have acquired over time, as discussed in chapter 4.

When we look out we don't see words above us saying *sky* and *clouds;* we see actual sky and clouds. Although there are worlds of abstract ideas, the grounding of all teaching and learning is lived sensory experience. One of the primary reasons what we teach may not make sense and students may not pay attention is that we provide words and symbols—we use dry language—without engaging the sensory modalities of learners.

One of the saddest features of much education is the extent to which it ignores the sensory nature of human experience. Schools that look and sound like prisons are quite literally deprived environments that grossly underutilize the sensory and perceptual capacities of students.

Activity 2: The Nature of Attention

We all know that attention is extremely important, and we see the label "attention deficit disorder" everywhere. However, if we seriously want to engage the attention of learners, we need to realize how multifaceted attention really is. There are at least two characteristics of attention. The first is that attention is selective. The second is the degree to which it is sustained.

Keep a notebook with you for, say, a few hours of a working day. As often as you can remember, record the events and incidents that attract your notice. Do your best to grasp what actually gained your attention and what actually led you to continue to attend or to shift focus to something else. Ask yourself questions such as these:

What did I really care about?

How much energy did I invest in attending?

What else was going on in my mind at the time?

What did it take for my attention to be diverted?

How important was novelty?

To what extent was my capacity to pay attention influenced by stress, excitement, health, or fatigue?

You might also reflect on the ways in which you constantly scanned the environment for what was going on.

Was there anything that you were on the lookout for?

Was there much going on that you simply ignored?

Commentary

Note that we live in a dynamic context in which people are interacting and events taking place that may be important to us but many of which cannot be controlled. The result is that we are constantly scanning our context, being attracted by outer events yet being driven by what interests and motivates us.

And what is true for each of us is true for every student we teach.

Exploring the Power of the Peripheral Context

The peripheral environment—that aspect of all that is going on that we do not directly attend to—can attract our attention. However, it can also influence us indirectly.

 Activity 3: Life Environments

For just a moment, think of your favorite restaurant. Now try to "feel" it. Pay particular attention to what makes this place special.

Is the food the only thing? What about the ambience? How do the food, service, setting, plus your memories all work together to make the place special? Discuss.

Are there any impressions that are real but are hard to put into words? Try drawing or moving to express to others the impressions that are vivid in your mind.

Reflect on the choice of the neighborhood in which you live.

To what extent have you selected it because it seems or feels right? What are the aspects of the neighborhood that create that sense for you?

Now reflect for a moment on how some of your friends and acquaintances have "orchestrated" their environments.

How do they use color, space, art, and artifacts? What about large corporations? Have you been anywhere where people who have more power also have larger offices or office space on higher floors in a building? What other peripheral indications of power and prestige do you see in corporations and government offices?

Commentary

> *Context matters! We need to recognize that we live and work in complex environments that are rich in signals, messages, and information, much of which is unarticulated and indirect. These messages influence attitudes and states of mind and, therefore, how much we will risk, how relaxed and caring we can be, how self-protective and mean we can be. Once we become sensitive to the environmental messages, we can begin to take charge of these peripheral messages.*

When safety and some sense of comfort are absent, for example, your natural survival mechanisms will become vigilant for potential danger (the signals that tell us we are not safe or comfortable may be extremely subtle or highly personal). We all have this reaction even though different reactions will be triggered by different situations for different individuals.

The opposite tends to be true, as well. When the peripheral messages spell safety and relaxation, we are more likely to be open to looking at our experiences in new and more creative ways.

 ### *Activity 4: School Environments*

Apply the thinking and notions you just explored in an evaluation of your school, classroom, and office. Ask what each observation tells you—what message the environment is conveying—to children and adults. Use the following questions as a guide:

What is the ratio of living plants to concrete, both inside and outside the building?

What is the ratio of closed to open spaces?

What sorts of relationships are there between the adults?

Do you hear singing anywhere (other than the music or choir room)?

How is time organized, and how are beginnings and endings of time periods signaled?

Is the environment joyful?

To what extent is the language of adults in the school filled with the subject matter that is taught in classes?

To what extent does the language of the adults reflect real expertise in specific fields?

To what extent does the language and behavior of adults indicate that reflection, critical thinking, high standards, and open minds are natural aspects of everyday life?

Commentary

> *The entire environment teaches, including the teacher as a person; the relation-ships between adults; the design of buildings; the atmosphere in the school and classroom; the use of light, sound, art, and music; the degree to which the environment is intellectually stimulating or relatively unthinking; and more. Content is never separate from context. You and the elements of the learning community may speak much louder than words or specific skills you teach.*

Georgi Lozanov (1978) suggests, in fact, that one of the key ingredients that helps students to learn is the prestige that teachers have in the eyes of their students. He is not talking power or fame. Rather, he says that prestige depends on genuine expertise and integrity, which are communicated indirectly—peripherally—but end up influencing the decisions we make about people and the importance of what they are saying.

Challenge for Practice

Peripheral stimuli are operating whether we like it or not. They are part of reality, and they contribute to the packaging of every message that a learner receives. They include "light," barely perceptible but nevertheless quite potent, stimuli. Hence, they contribute to the formation of dynamical knowledge.

The environment must be orchestrated in a way that frees our students and us from the influence of signals that inhibit learning. Generally speaking, art, classical music, living plants, orderly room arrangements, and visual stimuli affect us more positively than do disorder, blank walls, or disorganized decorations. Keeping the effect of peripheral elements in mind when we orchestrate our environments is important.

One key here is congruence. An administrator or a teacher who is basically uncaring or incompetent will not change that impression regardless of how many plants she puts in her office or what kind of classical music he plays.

A Question to Explore as a Learner

What do principle 7 and the ideas in this chapter suggest for your own learning?

Questions to Explore as an Educator

Do you have appropriate, gentle routines and procedures that orient students to your class and to specific tasks?

To what extent does your entire school demonstrate support for the kinds of values you all say you promote?

All in all, are students in a healthy, intellectually challenging environment where paying attention is natural?

Are the decorations, building, and grounds of your school conducive to learning and developing mentally and physically healthy citizens?

Do your classrooms and school activities give students experiences in democratic decision making?

What would your ideal school look like? Where can you begin to realize that vision?

To what extent is the content of your course actually lived in the place where it is taught? For example, do teachers actually use math and the tools of critical thinking in their everyday discussions? Are copies of great works of art found in "ordinary" places, such as the school office? Do adults in your school exhibit common rules of courtesy?

Is your local community involved in supporting school goals and functions? Do these goals include an appreciation of intellectual activities?

As you reflect on your discussions about the preceding questions, ask yourself these questions:

1. **How does principle 7 challenge your assumptions about learning?**

2. **How does principle 7 challenge your assumptions about teaching?**

3. **How does principle 7 challenge your assumptions about discipline?**

4. **How does principle 7 challenge your assumptions about assessment?**

What is, is always in process.

13

Learning Always Involves Conscious and Unconscious Processes

Otto Loewi, a great neuroscientist, came upon the existence of a fundamental brain substance called acetylcholine *in a dream. On the night before Easter Sunday in 1920, he awoke, made some notes, and went back to sleep. He could not later decipher what he had written. "The next night at three o'clock the idea returned. It was the design of an experiment to determine whether or not the hypothesis of chemical transmission I had uttered seventeen years ago was correct. I got up immediately, went to the laboratory, and performed a simple experiment on a frog heart according to the nocturnal design . . . These results unequivocally proved that the nerves do not influence the heart directly but liberate from their terminals specific chemical substances which, in their turn, cause the well-known modification of the function of the heart characteristic of the stimulation of its nerves."*

—R. Restak
Brainscapes

Loewi's experience is one of many in which profound insights have occurred to people in or after dreams, or at moments when they are engaged with something else entirely. Such experiences illustrate the fact that the brain/mind functions unconsciously as well as consciously. And it does so on many levels.

Note also the circumstances under which Loewi had his insight. He had been working passionately and diligently on a series of problems for a considerable period of time. He was also very well versed in his subject matter. In other words, he had been consciously and intentionally attending to an issue, which prepared and occupied his mind in some ways, even when he was not consciously addressing the issue. In effect, he was priming his unconsciousness. Then, when he somehow "let go," his unconscious processing took over.

One lesson we are learning is that meaningful learning and creative problem solving are actually different sides of the same coin; that is, a person who works extremely hard to understand something of great personal importance is also engaged in a creative process that culminates in an "aha" of insight. Such a process is very much like the construction of meaning, which involves multiple experiences that are processed until the point at which the student gets an "aha"—what we call "felt meaning" (see chapter 18).

You may have a student who for weeks doesn't seem to "get it." Then this student goes home over a break or talks with someone totally unrelated to school, and suddenly the light goes on. The student may have an "aha" experience.

As we point out in chapter 3, there are many levels of unconscious functioning. Much of therapy, beginning with Freud, is based on the fact that every human being is engaged in cognitive processes that are below the level of awareness. Psychologists are beginning to call this subconscious level of awareness implicit cognition. *At the same time, more and more research reveals that we can all become more aware of what is transpiring in our subconscious lives and that we can develop increased capacities to monitor and regulate ourselves. Even children are capable of becoming aware of their emotions to manage them more appropriately.*

One of our Park View Middle School teachers taught her emotionally disturbed special education students to manage their emotions. These students are in her regular classroom where she has created a "time out" area. Some of her students have learned to recognize when they are becoming emotionally volatile. They excuse themselves from whatever activity they are engaged in, go to the time out area, and take time to calm down and reflect, or ask her to help them understand what they are feeling. When they feel back in control, they return to the group.

One primary task of educators is to help students take charge of their conscious and unconscious processing. We can develop several core capacities to facilitate conscious and unconscious processing. One is becoming more mindful. Another is to tolerate active uncertainty, and a third is the capacity to orchestrate the environment so that it supports the ideas, themes, and issues being explored.

➤ *Activity 1: Developing Mindfulness*

One aspect of mindfulness is to have the time and awareness to note our inner state, to catch it, and to change our automatic response. A beautiful illustration comes from a student at Peninsula School. "When 10:15 came around sometimes, and math time came, I just kind of . . . whatcha call it, it's like a . . . a reaction of 'Oh, no, it's math. I don't want to do math.' But then . . . you know, it's just a kind of thing you do, and then I say, 'Wait a minute. Ease up. There's nothing wrong with it, so go ahead and do your math.' (laughs)" (Fadiman 1988).

This simple but powerful exercise has three parts. Take one or two minutes several times a day just to stop and observe what is happening all around you. For part of the time, allow your normal language and inner dialogue to describe what you observe. For part of the time do your best to observe without using language or labels to describe. You might like to experiment with this exercise for a week or two. Then, if it seems appropriate, spend a little time simply observing your own thoughts and emotional reactions.

What was easy? What was difficult? Did you observe any changes over time in the nature and quality of your experience? Did your awareness of your own inner working change in any way? Did your awareness of what was happening in your environment change in any way?

Commentary

If we really want to learn from experience then we need to master the art of experiencing fully. In this way we begin to discern nuances, implications, relationships, causes and effects, tendencies, patterns of behavior, and a fuller gamut of meanings and possibilities.

This exercise can become very helpful in teaching. Many students gloss over what is in front of them, which limits their ability to understand. While we are not advocating your use of this exercise with students, it can help you become more aware of their needs and of what is happening in the classroom.

 ### Activity 2: Active Uncertainty

To capitalize on the power of unconscious processing, we must use our conscious minds well and know how to keep the sort of open mind that allows new insights to form. Perhaps most critical is learning how to delay rushing to judgment and forming instant opinions. One of the best processes we know for helping adults open to other possibilities and acquire more tolerance for active uncertainty is the ordered sharing phase of your Mindshifts process group. Now might be a good time to review ordered sharing.

Do you do the ordered sharing as explained in chapter 5?

Has the process influenced the ways in which you listen to others? How?

Have the process and your group experience influenced the ways in which you listen to yourself? How?

Do you take more time to work on ideas and strategies that you have not yet mastered?

Is it easier to accept the opinions of others as legitimate?

Commentary

According to Langer (1989), "Mindlessness is the rigid reliance on old categories; mindfulness means the continual creation of new ones" (63). Thus, a central aspect of the work of educators is to engender a capacity for "active uncertainty" in students and in ourselves. This uncertainty includes the ability to accept uncertainty, tolerate ambiguity, and welcome new insights. It is extremely important that we create an atmosphere in which different opinions, others' perceptions, and not knowing and being confused are perceived as a positive experience. Such an atmosphere creates the gates through which we pass from what was known to new learning.

There is a difference between having an open mind and thinking that we have an open mind. Each of us is—or has—a Self; we have acquired an extensive set of values and beliefs that define what we regard as real and important. Students also have such a set of beliefs. Our tendency is to deny or reject what conflicts with our inner reality, or to reduce what is new to fit in with what we already know. Becoming open to more possibilities is vital to learning and teaching.

➤ *Activity 3: Creative Problem Solving*

There is an interplay between conscious and unconscious, as demonstrated by Loewi's experience. Our job is to help our students use both. It may help to refer to one of the basic models that has been developed for creative problem solving.

In creative problem solving, the goal is to engage intentionally and consciously in several processes that will "prime" the unconscious to come up with an insightful answer. The technique we describe provides an overview of how it is done.

We invite you to experiment with the following procedure.

Step 1: Identify a manageable problem of interest to you that needs an insightful solution. Talk it through, discuss it, write it down, express it in various ways.

Step 2: Gather all the information about the problem you can. Ask questions. Talk to people. Read books. Watch videos. Observe people and events.

Step 3: Elaborate creatively. Find a variety of ways to think about and experience the problem and the information. Go to the top of a tall building and think about perspective. Play with a map of the world and think about interconnectedness. Pretend to be various people and think about various points of view.

Step 4: Incubate. Leave the problem alone in your mind for a while, even though doing so can be very difficult. Sometimes you need to get so involved in something else that you actually do not have the time or energy to bother about your problem. Sometimes it is a matter of simply taking a break—exercise, relax, go to a movie, garden. Sometimes it is a matter of consciously giving yourself permission to think about other things —for an hour, a week, or longer. In practice, good problem solvers often consciously revisit problems, often in settings different from those in which the problem arose. They may be in a restaurant, on the beach, at a party, or in some other setting. Feel free to revisit your problem occasionally, but be sure you take some genuine time away from the problem, too.

Step 5: Be awake to the "aha!" solutions that emerge. You may have a dream in which an insight is embedded. You may overhear a remark in a conversation that points the way. You may be singing in the shower when an idea comes to mind. You may get lots of insights. Make a point of noting them, perhaps in a small notebook you keep with you. Or record your dreams when you wake up.

Step 6: Test the insight. The test may be difficult because your idea may be contrary to conventional wisdom. Find ways to try it out in practice and discuss it with people who you know have open and questioning minds.

Commentary

Educators can use the problem-solving process we describe to solve problems about school, but it also carries with it hints about how to help students learn complex material. For instance, we can help them to formulate questions of real, personal interest. We can help them to analyze and talk about their questions. We can introduce relevant works of art and music (among other things) to help prime their unconscious. We can help them have and process relevant experiences, and more. The key is to grasp the ways in which they and we can work together to help them take charge of their conscious and unconscious processing.

Challenge to Practice

Psychologists have known for a long time that learning is assisted by deep processing. In the final chapters of the book we introduce the notion of active processing as the art of helping students capitalize on experience.

One foundation of active processing is assisting students to become more mindful. Another is to help them keep an open mind. And of course, for us to help them effectively, we need to be adept ourselves.

A Question to Explore as a Learner

What do principle 8 and the ideas in this chapter suggest for your own learning?

Questions to Explore as an Educator

Do your students ever suddenly show that they learned something when you were beginning to doubt that it had sunk in?

Do student understandings ever show up in unexpected contexts?

Do you ever ask questions or generate projects that lead to ongoing student interest over a long period of time? When do these questions work and when don't they?

How aware of their own learning styles and processes are your students? How do you know?

How aware are you of what actually happens in your class or work environment? How do you know?

As you reflect on your discussions about the preceding questions, ask yourself these questions:

1. **How does principle 8 challenge your assumptions about learning?**

2. **How does principle 8 challenge your assumptions about teaching?**

3. **How does principle 8 challenge your assumptions about discipline?**

4. How does principle 8 challenge your assumptions about assessment?

Everything is separate and connected.

14

We Have at Least Two Ways of Organizing Memory

Recently, Geoffrey and Renate were in Australia. While we were in Sydney, people kept talking about Homebush, the site of the year 2000 Olympics. Despite others' descriptions, we could not get a sense of the place—it remained a name. So one day we visited. We took a ferry, a jet cat, up the Parramatta River, and transferred to a bus that took us around the site and gave a view of the whole complex. At the visitor's center we embarked on a tour by foot. We visited the aquatic center, gazed at the multiple pools, including the one with a movable floor and the children's pools, had coffee in a small restaurant, and browsed through the gift shop. Leaving the aquatic center, we turned the wrong way and found ourselves on a limited-access road in a hard-hat area—one that gave us a unique perspective of the sports complex that was still under construction. To exit, we had to climb over some barriers and ended up near a large building being used for the Royal Easter Show (the state fair). We finally found our way back to the visitor's center, viewed the exhibits, looked at a map to see where we had been, and took the bus and ferry back to Sydney.

Memory is quite a complex phenomenon. There are many different theories about how memory works, and several possible memory systems have been identified. They include memories of facts (declarative memories), routines and procedures (procedural memory), events (episodic memory), meanings (semantic memory), and emotional memories. The challenge for educators is to find a way of thinking about memory that results in a practical tool without having to address all the systems separately.

We have found the model of memory developed by O'Keefe and Nadel (1978) the most powerful and effective because it integrates the various memory systems. They make the basic distinction between rote learning and lived experience, and you can use that distinction in education. The distinction is formulated in terms of what they call taxon memory (from taxonomies) and locale memory (from location in space).

Geoffrey and Renate had a real experience that employed their locale memory system. In the course of their tour, information (facts usually stored in declarative memory) was naturally embedded, the facts were given meaning in context (semantic memory), which depended partly on their emotional engagement (emotional memory). And when the experience was over, they stored it as an entire event (episodic memory). At the same time, they practiced some routines and procedures, such as the right way to pay fare and board the ferry (procedural memory), but the rehearsal took place in an ongoing context and so remained meaningful. It is this integrated use of modes of memory that makes learning easier and more powerful. That is why mastering the differences and relationships between rote memory and experiential memory is so important.

Taxon Memory Systems: Rote Memory

The brain has some systems that are designed for learning by rote, and some rote memorization is essential for success and survival, whether it be a password in the army or a way to look before crossing a busy street. Taxon systems have several properties:

- **Facts and skills are stored by practice and rehearsal.** A golfer practices her swing and a firefighter practices rescues for very good reasons. The essential elements need to be automatic.

- **The taxon systems tend to fatigue, so intervals of rest are necessary.** Intervals can be brief (perhaps a few minutes each hour). Waiting a few days before reviewing is also effective in some situations, which is the reason some teachers recommend that a student review material two nights in a row, then wait until one week later.

- **The taxon systems can be intrinsically motivated** (as when we decide to remember a phone number) **and extrinsically motivated,** such as through imposed rewards and punishments (as when students try to remember facts to avoid failing a test).

- **The items that are stored can be separated from one another** and may have little or no meaning to the learner. For instance, students might remember who painted the *Mona Lisa* or the dates of the Boer War, even if they could care less about the facts.

- **Sometimes the memories can be stored relatively quickly and unintentionally,** for instance, during some intense emotional experiences. Thus flying through a storm may be enough to create a phobic response to flying.

One very important result that applies to education is that standardized tests can be created to test only for facts and procedures that are stored in taxon systems.

Locale Memory: Spatial, Autobiographical Memory

The locale system records our moment-to-moment life experience. According to O'Keefe and Nadel (1978), it is designed to register where we are in space and to register the unfolding story of what happens to us, as happened with Geoffrey and Renate in Australia.

Regardless of what we focus on at any moment, the brain processes the entire context within which our focusing is taking place. Without knowing it, you are organizing an enormous number of signals and stimuli in the form of an ongoing life story. In addition to whatever activity has your attention, and in addition to monitoring the environment, your brain/mind is also recording a total experience.

The locale system has several properties:

- **It is almost inexhaustible.** It operates from morning to night for a lifetime. (Except, perhaps, when you might have been totally exhausted, has there ever been a time when you have been in a new place and made *no* attempt to orient yourself?)

- **Because it must adjust to new situations immediately it is innately motivated by novelty.** (Do you ever spontaneously pay attention to significant events or new people that move into your life?)

- **The locale system calls upon all the mind/body systems.** The quality and duration of the maps are very greatly influenced by sensory awareness and emotional intensity. The more *present* and *emotionally engaged* we are in some context, the more complete is the map. (Is there an emotional event in your past that you still remember very vividly?)

- **The core of the locale system is that it builds relationships among facts, events, and experiences.** It is a contextual memory system.

One very important result that applies to education is that the relationships that are registered by the locale memory system can be demonstrated by appropriate reactions in spontaneous, natural, real-world situations.

Exploring Memory

Our challenge is to determine how the two systems work together and how to best employ them in education.

➤ ## Activity 1: Taxon Systems and Rote Learning

We invite you to memorize the names of some of the kings of England, using the following doggerel:

> *Willy, Willy, Harry, Ste,*
>
> *Harry, Dick, John, Harry III.*
>
> *1, 2, 3 Neds, Richard 2,*
>
> *Henry 4, 5, 6, then who?*

Test yourself. Can you remember?

Did you want to remember the doggerel?

Have you ever had to learn some facts by rote? How did you do it? What was it that tied them together for you?

Have you ever had to learn a procedure by rote (such as booting up a computer or getting on the Internet)? How did you do it?

Have you ever been required to learn a subject or skill by rote?

Do you still remember facts that were never of practical use to you?

What initially meaningless memories have you stored that have ultimately become meaningful?

In what circumstances might this form of learning be important and valuable? For instance, have you ever had to remember a route from one place to another in a new city? Or how to boot up a computer or start a machine that you did not understand? Or master some safety requirements? Or remember information such as parts of the body that you knew would become more meaningful later?

Commentary

Practice and rehearsal work. There are strategies that make it easier and more effective. We can test in a variety of ways to see if we have stored the material. And we can call upon the facts and procedures at almost any time. However, in general, all that we have is the facts or procedures that we remember. There is little additional relationship between them, and if we do nothing more than memorize, the facts and procedures tend to be useless in solving complex, real-world problems.

Memories that are stored in taxon systems tend to be automatic and repeatable even under pressure. They do not need to make sense. In fact, one of the interesting things about taxon systems is that they can be programmed very much like a computer to produce the same response over and over, unconnected to other information, to the context, or to ongoing events. This characteristic of taxon systems can be extremely valuable. We want firefighters, for instance, to have a repertoire of automatic responses that are available anywhere, anytime.

This type of memorization is behind much of the orthodox approach to testing and assessing students, as is particularly evident in multiple-choice questions. Education as a system is designed to rely on taxon learning. The problem is that our brain has storage limits, and these limits can be quite severe. For example, rote learning engages memory for the short term, but the brain has a limited capacity to learn from context while it is memorizing something. Even if information is moved into long-term memory, the thing that may be lost is the relationship between facts and procedures in a lived context.

➤ Activity 2: Locale Memory and Everyday Experience

Next time you go to the mall, to a movie, or to school, spend a few moments afterward recollecting the events that led up to your activity. The following illustrative questions may help you:

Whom were you with?

What was the weather like?

How did you travel?

Where did you park (if you parked)?

How easy was it to get a sense of the layout so that, for instance, you could find the restroom, then find your way back?

What mood were you in?

Of what story in your life was this incident a part?

Commentary

As you move through the mall, school, or other place, a basic "map" or picture of how everything was related falls into place instantly and naturally. That is, you find your way around without much effort. If the location is very complex, developing the map takes some time and some work, but it is rarely merely a matter of memorization. Rather it is a matter of paying attention to landmarks and where things are in relation to other things, such as a mall exit being near a health food store. And the more attentive and engaged you are at the time, the more things you will remember later. The key point is that you are living an experience in space and time, and it naturally becomes a part of the story of your life if you find it sufficiently interesting.

Activity 3: Combining Rote Learning and More Complex Experience

Imagine that you really want to understand the early history of England and the nature of royalty. There is a mystery series written by Ellis Peters about a twelfth-century monk named Cadfael. He solves murders in much the same manner as does a modern sleuth, but his stories, clues, and characters resonate with and are richly colored by the time in which he lives. For instance, he lives when Stephen and his cousin Maude were competing for the throne of England, and his clues are the flowers and herbs of the time. For those who enjoy mysteries, simply being engaged in the story provides a context within which some of the kings and queens of England will be naturally embedded in memory and remembered later.

We suggest that you purchase one or two of the books or watch the mystery series. Then discuss what you have learned about the British royalty of the time.

Commentary

Memorization provides some structure, some rails to run along. However, reading adds detail and fleshes out relationships. You will be much better equipped to talk about the time and to understand the tortured nature of English royal relationships if you read the mysteries than if you had simply memorized the names of the royal figures. You will also have developed usable, dynamical maps by giving yourself and students similar contexts—and over time, if you were to learn more about royalty in other experiential ways, you could easily recall pertinent material you learned from your previous reading. But you would also know a great deal of additional information. Note also that all types of memory need to be consolidated. Locale memories are consolidated with multiple exposures and experiences sparked by memory. They may include some practice and rehearsal but are never limited to that.

➤ ### *Activity 4: Understanding the Ways You Have Already Combined the Memory Systems*

Think of some field or activity (a hobby or second job, perhaps) that you have explored or worked on for a considerable period, either recently or in the past. Ideally, you will choose one that has posed a real challenge to you, but in which you acquired some mastery.

Did you receive any direct instruction or training?

In how many life events and incidents has your hobby figured in some way?

How much practice and rehearsal did you do and in what contexts?

To what extent did novelty keep you going?

To what extent have you discussed this interest with others?

To what extent have you been exposed to aspects of it in various ways, often inadvertently (movies, chance discussions, magazines and journals, friends and colleagues)?

How much and what types of real-world performance of your hobby have you experienced?

To what extent is your mastery reflected in the fact that you can now recall new information about the field very quickly?

Commentary

Learning for real-world competence is messy. We tend to need some intrinsic motivation, a personal interest and drive. We tend to have multiple experiences that slowly begin to merge into complex maps and patterns over time, especially when we analyze, reflect on, and process the experiences. We need to practice and rehearse a significant amount, but we will do so in a variety of ways and will usually find it meaningful. Every now and again a novel situation will occur, and we will test the experience to see how it fits with what we already know. In the course of all these events, we will have a great deal of sensory input and will experience a wide range of emotions. Over time, the various aspects of the hobby become connected and related to one another, and we are able to call upon various aspects of our knowing in a variety ways. We end up with genuinely usable memories.

Challenge for Practice

We need both memory systems. In fact, the two systems interact all the time in the natural operation of the brain. It is important that we grasp their different properties very clearly, because the conditions we set up will determine how effectively learners use the two systems. The key is to master the art of embedding new information and skills in the context of sufficiently real and complex experience.

We do not want robots that execute rote recitations of course content. Ultimately we want people to have complex, flexible maps of life that allow them to change course if the context requires it. To do that, students must look for meaningfulness, which requires them to use their locale memory system in conjunction with new information.

A Question to Explore as a Learner

What do principle 9 and the ideas in this chapter suggest for your own learning?

Questions to Explore as an Educator

How do you help students link to and build on what they already know?

To what extent do you provide or make possible complex experiences in which new subjects and information are embedded?

Do students have the opportunity to engage in authentic discussion about what they are studying? How do you know the discussions are authentic?

What percentage of your instruction involves pure practice and rehearsal?

Based on what you know of the two memory systems, what percentage would be appropriate?

What sorts of tests do you administer? What aspects of memory do you think you are testing?

As you reflect on your discussions about the preceding questions, ask yourself these questions:

1. **How does principle 9 challenge your assumptions about learning?**

2. **How does principle 9 challenge your assumptions about teaching?**

3. **How does principle 9 challenge your assumptions about discipline?**

4. **How does principle 9 challenge your assumptions about assessment?**

Rhythms and cycles are present everywhere.

15

Learning Is Developmental

In the middle of that gray month Emelina's youngest son learned to walk. I was alone with him when it happened . . . For quite a while now Nicholas had been cruising the perimeters of his world, walking confidently from house to tree to lawn chair to wall, so long as he had something to hold on to. Sometime what he touched was nothing more than apparent security . . . He spotted a hummingbird . . . Nicholas wanted it . . . he took one step and then another, buoyed up by some impossible antigravity . . . I stayed out there with my book for the rest of the afternoon, surreptitiously watching as he tried it over and over. He was completely undeterred by failure. The motivation packed in that small body was a miracle to see. I wished I could bottle that passion for accomplishment and squeeze out some of the elixir, a drop at a time, on my high school students. They would move mountains.

—Barbara Kingsolver
Animal Dreams

While the basic structure of the brain is genetically programmed to develop, one awe-inspiring feature is that much of the electrical activity, the growth of dendritic branches on neurons, the synaptic connections between neurons, the formation of the myelin sheath that coats neurons and helps to accelerate the transmission of signals, and much more are all influenced by experience.

As Diamond and Hopson (1998) note, "The emerging message is clear: The brain, with its complex architecture and limitless potential, is a highly plastic, constantly changing entity that is powerfully shaped by our experiences in childhood and throughout life" (2).

As educators we need to understand that we are not just *stuffing* students' brains with facts. Rather, we are helping them develop clusters of neurons that fire at the same time, the result of which is the emergence of ever larger and more complex neural networks that reflect the acquisition of skills and ideas tied to purposes and meanings. The term used to describe the way the brain changes in response to experience is *plasticity*.

Critical periods are apparent in human development. Vision is one example. People who are blind from birth and have surgery to restore their sight many years later never acquire full vision because their brains have not been properly wired. Language is another example. So-called wolf children who are not exposed to human speech for the first twelve or so years of life never acquire full linguistic capacity. However, critical periods are not precise, and the research is still not clear enough for us to make many specific recommendations.

A great deal of evidence also indicates that some brain plasticity lasts throughout life. Elderly people can master a new language (even though the ear for accent is usually diminished).

The research shows that for brain development to be optimized, people need to be immersed in enriched environments. One of our major challenges as educators is to understand the nature of enrichment and to grasp how to capitalize on patterns of development.

Exploring Human Development

There are many aspects of human development. We touch on just a few of them to convey a sense of the complexity involved.

➤ *Activity 1: Building Foundations*

In the very early years, emotion and feeling are paramount. Children need an environment that is stimulating. At the same time, it must be safe and caring. Even after the age of three, children need this foundation. While we cannot control or even perhaps affect what parents and the wider community do with our students, at the very least educators should honor these basic needs in students. Answering the following questions will help you do so.

What do we mean by *stimulation, safety,* and *caring*? For example, one aspect of safety is consistency. Would you have included that criterion in your definition?

What indicators would tell you that the qualities described in the first item were actually present in your place of work?

What, in particular, is the relationship between what people say and what they do? Is the fact that we say we care about children necessarily reflected in what we do?

How might the interactions among adults influence children's experience?

Commentary

Note that even though we were talking specifically about ideal environments for infants and young children in the explanation, the same qualities and characteristics apply to professionals in every educational environment to some extent. Adults as well as children need safe environments that support taking risks in thinking, acting, and learning.

 ## *Activity 2: Enrichment of Experience*

One of the most exciting findings in brain research was originally reported by a group of researchers at University of California at Berkeley (Diamond, Krech, and Rosenzweig 1964). Over a period of roughly forty years, they studied the anatomical features of rats' brains. Quite by accident, they discovered that the brains of rats living in what came to be known as *enriched environments* weighed more than the brains of rats in *impoverished environments*. This research has been replicated in many parts of the world.

The impoverished conditions are constituted by individual cages with solid walls; the animals cannot see or touch one another. The cages are in separate, quiet, dimly lit rooms. In the enriched environments, the rats are housed in groups of ten to twelve, in large cages, and they have toys including ladders, wheels, boxes, platforms, and so on, which are changed regularly. The cages are in large, brightly lit rooms. Super-enriched environments are those in which rats have thirty-minute exploratory sessions each day in large outdoor fields in groups of five or six, with barriers constructed in patterns that change daily. It is important to note that the most enriching environment for the rats appears to be their natural habitat.

The challenge resulting from this research is to understand adequately what constitutes enrichment for people. We begin by calling upon our collective experience.

In what sort of musical environment do you think Mozart was immersed as a youngster?

What sorts of physical and social experiences do you think tend to occur in the lives of those who become great athletes?

How would you characterize the differences in the homes of children who learn to read quickly and those who don't take to reading at all?

How would you account for those people who develop competencies that seem to be totally at odds with the environments in which they grow up?

Commentary

For the purposes of education, we can no longer afford to separate brain/mind development from life experience. Although many implications still need to be worked out, the bottom line is that experience changes the physiological structure and operation of our brains. Thus environments need to be complex, stimulating, and safe. However, we must consider this point with some caution, because it is not necessarily true that a person from a home with lots of toys will have a more highly developed brain than a person who plays in the streets. There are so many factors that most children are likely to be impoverished in some ways and enriched in others.

Activity 3: Zone of Proximal Development

Lev Vygotsky (1978) suggests that in all student-teacher interactions, a zone of proximal development exists, that is, the capacity of the teacher matches the students' expanding capacities. Of course, sometimes students fool us. They are often much more capable of understanding than we believe. Indeed, one reason many students are a discipline problem or drop out altogether is that they are not challenged to proceed at a rate at which they are capable.

An additional problem is that learning and human development are nonlinear and messy. There are forward, backward, and sideways steps even as there is general growth. And it usually takes a fairly complex, lifelike environment to assess accurately what sort of progress a person is making.

Answer the following questions:

How do you assess a student's readiness? How do you test your own methods and means of assessment so that you can trust them?

Have you ever seen a presentation or program that so patronized you (underestimated your abilities or knowledge), you ignored it, even if you had been told it was important for your future? How might you relate this experience to that of students in a classroom?

Has your own development in any field been messy and nonlinear? How did you handle it? If others were teaching or guiding you, how did they handle it? Were you satisfied with what happened?

Commentary

A zone of proximal development is not an objectively identifiable phenomenon. The extent to which a given teacher can help a given learner depends a great deal on their perceptions and capacity to relate to each other, on the teacher's expertise and competence, on the student's competence and background, on the context, and on other factors.

These factors have an important bearing on high standards. Research and our own experience combine to suggest that those who best inspire high-standard performances in students are those who actually live by those standards themselves and do not just give them lip service. For example, students need to see you using critical thinking skills, not simply requiring it in a classroom exercise. Similarly, students need to see you persevere to do so themselves. You can even nurture students' desire to learn itself by allowing them to see that you clearly love to learn and that you do not know it all.

➤ *Activity 4: Building and Growing*

Each of us is constantly building and renewing by relating the new to what we already know. In some ways, we just add more information and enrich what our brain has already established. Some language development fits this pattern. Sometimes helping a student is just a matter of connecting something new, such as geometry, to something he already loves, such as dance or perspective in art.

There are also multiple stages of human development. Some depend on increased maturity. Others depend on bringing additional abilities and capacities, such as the ability to use the abstract elements of ideas, theories, and symbols, on line.

Answer the following questions:

Have you ever learned something that had been puzzling you for a long time until someone showed you a way of relating it to something else that you knew quite well? How did you do it?

In what area are you becoming more competent and knowledgeable by building on what you already know?

Can you recall a time when you (perhaps suddenly) acquired a new capacity or ability? What happened? How did you feel?

Commentary

There are many aspects of intellectual and personal development. For instance, one aspect of human development is the capacity to engage in possibility thinking, to be able to deal with alternatives and see beyond black and white, right and wrong. Note that some of these capacities are not merely intellectual; they involve developing and refining awareness of ourselves and of the world we inhabit.

Challenge for Practice

In the early years the infant and young child are still becoming whole persons. Everything about them interacts as the self develops. They absorb everything in their experience—what we say, what we do, and what we are. Everything that we do in their early lives will influence them, so, as much as possible, we need to integrate into our practice and into our being the qualities that we want them to develop.

In later years, even though an identity has emerged somewhat, adolescents still integrate the content of what they experience with the quality of what they experience. Hence we continue to be called upon to function at and beyond the level we seek to develop in them.

A Question to Explore as a Learner

What do principle 10 and the ideas in this chapter suggest for your own learning?

Questions to Explore as an Educator

To what extent do you rely on students' age or grade to decide what is possible for them to learn or do?

Candace Pert claims in *Molecules of Emotion* that she has the ability to deal with paradox and possibility because she is a woman; does gender really make this sort of difference? A growing body of work deals with gender differences, ranging from Debra Blum's *Sex on the Brain* (1997) to Belenky, Clinchy, Goldberger, and Tarule's *Women's Ways of Knowing* (1986). They might be fruitful sources for discussion, with practical implications for single-sex schools and gender differences in maturation.

Is it possible to be open to possibilities yet have an appropriate sense of what is right and wrong? How do you deal with this issue in your personal life? How do you deal with this issue in your work with students, colleagues, and others?

As you reflect on your discussions about the preceding questions, ask yourself these questions:

1. **How does principle 10 challenge your assumptions about learning?**

2. **How does principle 10 challenge your assumptions about teaching?**

3. How does principle 10 challenge your assumptions about discipline?

4. How does principle 10 challenge your assumptions about assessment?

Stable systems resist change; dynamic systems exist by changing.

16

Complex Learning Is Enhanced by Challenge and Inhibited by Threat Associated with a Sense of Helplessness or Fatigue

If "normal" scientists are motivated by their work, revolutionary scientists—the ones who break away from existing theoretical paradigms to form new ones—are even more driven by enjoyment.

The rapt concentration on the child's face as she learns each new skill is a good indication of what enjoyment is about. And each instance of enjoyable learning adds to the complexity of the child's developing self.

Every flow activity provides a sense of discovery, a creative feeling of transporting the person into a new reality. It pushes the person to higher levels of performance, and leads to previously undreamed of states of consciousness. In short, it transforms the self by making it more complex. In this growth of the self lies the key to flow activities.

—Mihalyi Csikszentmihalyi
Flow (135, 47, 74)

In Csikszentmihalyi's words we find the sheer joy that makes much learning an end in itself. It does not have to be imposed, forced, or otherwise externally motivated. At the same time, joy is accompanied by the growth and increasing complexity of a person. In essence, working toward deep understanding and high standards is intrinsically exhilarating—when the conditions are right.

Of course, not all learning is joyful. Indeed, there are times when we all need simply to grit our teeth and keep going. The key, then, is for learners to be willing and able to grit their teeth—to persevere when necessary—even when the task is complex and understanding is difficult. This persistence is precisely what sets great scientists and artists apart from average ones.

Research shows that one of the key ingredients for demanding complex learning is high challenge. Now the word challenge *is ambiguous. Many people take it to mean that someone—perhaps a leader or educator—has a high expectation of learners and calls upon them to work harder and aim higher. There is some truth to that. More important, however, is the* inner *aspect of challenge. One quality of inner challenge is personal engagement, which begins with the learner's search for meaning (principle 3) and is generally referred to as* intrinsic *motivation. A second and indispensable quality is a sense of self-efficacy, which is the belief that success is possible as a result of one's own efforts. The goal for educators must be to create the conditions that elicit this personal aspect of high challenge in learners.*

Support for this notion of high challenge can be found in many sources, including research on stress and creativity. In his original work on stress, for instance, Hans Selye (1978) shows that there is a difference between *eustress* (from "euphoria"), which is the stress associated with creative tension, and the more harmful *distress* (from the Latin *dis,* which means bad, as in "disagreement"). Deci and Ryan (1987) list a set of qualities that are at the heart of creativity:

- autonomy
- great interest
- low pressure and tension
- positive emotional tone
- high self-esteem
- trust
- great persistence of behavior change
- physical and emotional health

We also know that intrinsic motivation can be undermined, that people can become deflated and uninvolved, and that the sense of Self can be diminished when people feel helpless or excessively fatigued or bored. This state is what Les Hart (1978) originally called being downshifted. Downshifting results in less-than-optimal performance and tends to happen when a particular set of conditions occurs; these conditions are, unfortunately present in much of traditional education.

Exploring High Challenge

Many factors contribute to intrinsic motivation. We invite you to reflect on activities and aspects of your life in which you have experienced challenge and flow.

 ## *Activity 1: Personal Desire to Learn or Accomplish*

Stories of people consumed by personal interest abound. They range from the ten-year-old in England who runs a successful antique business to athletes such as John Newcombe, who knew at a very early age that he wanted to win Wimbledon. They include great scientists and artists who pursue their passions, sometimes in the midst of extremely trying conditions.

Recall a time in your life when you had (or currently have) such a desire or interest. From where did it spring?

What made it so consuming?

How was the interest nurtured (if it was)?

To what extent did you acquire a deep personal interest in something because someone told you that it would be important to you later in life?

What interests are the result of another person's introducing them to you?

Commentary

By definition, intrinsic motivation comes from inside a person. However, it may be triggered or sparked by something that someone else says or does. It is possible to ignite another person's intrinsic motivation, but it is impossible to compel another person to be interested in something.

➤ *Activity 2: The Role of Self-Efficacy*

Csikszentmihalyi points out that the people who experience
flow are both challenged and competent in some field.
There is a difference, however, between the sort of self-
esteem that is expressed in feel-good language (such as "I
feel good about my math ability") and the sort of self-esteem
reflected in well-founded confidence in one's own ability to
solve a problem or perform a skill. The latter shows up in
what one does, but may even be accompanied by the
language of self-doubt (as with the really good math student
who says, "I am only so-so in math").

**Reflect on some aspect of your life in which you are at least moderately
skilled and others know that you are skilled. What are the indicators that
you are skilled?**

Are you a good judge of how skilled and competent you are?

**Do you ever just take it for granted that you can accomplish significant
tasks and projects involving your skill?**

Did you have to work hard to become skilled?

Commentary

Interest and self-efficacy reinforce each other. The combination leads to student empowerment. Unfortunately, many educators have been led to believe that praising someone for their effort is the primary source of self-efficacy. It is not. The experience of authentic success is vital. However, creating the conditions for actual success is difficult. It requires us to give students genuine choices. It requires some sort of scaffolding so that students can be supported as they learn to take charge. It requires a grasp of the developmental nature of learning (see principle 11).

Downshifting: The Antithesis of High Challenge

Some people have minds that are like steel rods—they persist and believe in themselves no matter what. For the majority of us, however, conditions can cause us to lose confidence in ourselves and our capacity to learn and accomplish. In short, we downshift. Geoffrey and Renate Caine (1994) have defined downshifting as a psychophysiological response to threat accompanied by or associated with a sense of helplessness or fatigue. The notion is derived from research in many fields, including the neurosciences, stress theory, creativity, self-efficacy, and sports psychology. The result is that we revert to early programmed responses and lose access to more rational brain functioning. We should add that people downshift in different ways. The consequence, however, is that downshifting limits their ability to choose their behavior, which inhibits new learning.

We suggest, on the basis of our research documented in *Making Connections: Teaching and the Human Brain,* that there is a set of conditions that educators and society create in education that lead to students' downshifting.

What Happens When We Downshift?

- **We seek to protect ourselves.** In the classroom, self-protection translates into pleasing the teacher, which translates into memorizing for the test rather than exploring and questioning to understand. The effect is to inhibit rather than to encourage meaningful learning.

- **We tend to have a significantly reduced capacity to adapt to new circumstances.** We tend to perseverate—to persist with set modes of behavior in a fairly rigid and unresponsive way. Students may therefore perpetuate ways of behaving and methods of study that do not work. In fact they tend to fail to respond to, and may not even perceive, substantial changes in the behavior of and signals from others. They may also daydream and lack the ability to focus.

- **We revert to routines, procedures, and behaviors that have been deeply programmed, usually in childhood.** Examples include ignoring others, procrastination, avoidance, and overt impatience. Reversion to such routine behaviors is particularly harmful because of what can be called "active uncertainty," which includes a capacity to tolerate ambiguity, is reduced.

- **We revert to a set of very primitive instinctual behaviors having to do with preservation of our safety.** The result is that in addition to bonding with others who are like minded (which we all do), we also become territorial and adversarial, treating others as the enemy, which is a large contributor to the discipline problems we find in school.

➤ *Activity 3: Ongoing Evaluation of Learning*

We invite you to read through the following conditions and ask, "To what extent are these conditions present in my school, classroom, and place of work?" Note that your intentions do not matter. What matters are the actual conditions you create or that exist. Notice especially the use of power and the power differential between student and teacher. Notice that the conditions tend to act almost invisibly to create students' sense of helplessness.

- **Prespecified "correct" outcomes have been established by an agent other than the learner.** This condition translates into students having to learn the answers the teacher has determined to be correct, which significantly narrows the available options of exploration. Students are not in charge of their own learning and therefore feel some degree of helplessness.

- **Personal meaning is limited.** What is to be learned does not connect with what students already know or want to know, which forces them into mere memorization; the brain deals with such information differently from the way in which it deals with meaningful information. Students' innovative, chosen ways of dealing with problems and situations are largely ignored.

- **Rewards and punishment are externally controlled and relatively immediate.** The consequences of action, including testing and grades, are not under the control of the students.

- **Restrictive time lines are given.** While deadlines are important in their place, a constant barrage of time limitations determined by others drives people to do what has to be done to meet the deadline, rather than to reflect on options or focus on the genuine parameters of the task.

- **Work to be done is relatively unfamiliar and little support is available.** Although some people work well alone and tackle new ideas and projects easily, for most people, isolation and/or endeavors unrelated to what they already know can exacerbate uncertainty and provide no reassurance that success is likely.

Commentary

It is easy to see that these conditions contribute synergistically to mere compliance by most students. We see individuals responding to the conditions acting largely from a state of helplessness and an inability to access their own motivation. This helplessness is largely grounded in the power differential between teacher and student. The conditions are situation specific, however. Students can feel various degrees of competence and helplessness in various contexts. It is also clear that people are different. Thus, some students perform very well in the conditions listed above. Sadly, some of our "best" students master this system and actually dislike open-ended and innovative approaches that maximize the making of creative connections.

The problem is complex because the conditions for learning are influenced in many different ways. For example, a school may establish a pervasive set of conditions that tend to operate generally, but sometimes they can be neutralized or limited in a specific class with a very good teacher.

Another problem is that a person who is chronically downshifted may also become extremely sensitive to any new source of stress. The nervous systems of some students may be in a constant state of vigilance, making creative risk taking and higher-order thinking almost impossible.

Thus, many conditions that educators take for granted are actually self-defeating. The reliance on tests that are unrelated to meaning or that ignore complex performance, the overreliance on grades and consequences, the use of time lines that suit administration but not learning, and other factors tend to lead many, and perhaps most, students to downshift. The result is that they become less capable of meeting the higher standards that are being demanded. We should add that the adults, teachers, and other staff in the system can and do downshift as well.

The hidden conditions that inhibit learning in the classroom can also be expected to operate in the restructuring of an organization. While the circumstances vary from school to school and district to district, there are obvious common parallels to the classroom situation. Schools are often expected to take a specific shape and to provide quite specific results in the face of externally controlled tests and criteria of excellence. Test scores are a current example. Such emphasis on accountability established by outside agencies carries with it the threat of severe punishment, including the threat of losing a job. Such requirements force many teachers to follow traditional methods of teaching at a time when innovation and risk taking are called for.

Challenge to Practice

Educators need to walk a fine line between exercising their power and empowering students. We need to tap into students' intrinsic motivation and yet call for them to work on and learn what society mandates. We need to assess their learning, but must also master the art of engaging them in authentic self-assessment. We have some time constraints, and yet we have to provide appropriate amounts of time for genuine work to be done and learning to occur. We need to provide feedback or make it available, and yet create conditions in which it is safe for students to take risks. All of these conditions are difficult but essential to implement.

A Question to Explore as a Learner

What do principle 11 and the ideas in this chapter suggest for your own learning?

Questions to Explore as an Educator

In what ways can one discern or recognize genuine student interest? What indicators might you use? One of ours is the extent to which students continue working after they no longer "have" to.

How does one reconcile "right answers" with genuine room for alternatives?

What sorts of time parameters make it possible for intrinsic motivation to thrive?

How does one help students assess their own competence accurately?

How does one empower students while managing the class responsibly?

How do we arrange our work so that we either engage or develop the natural interests of students and connect these with the syllabus? What ways of so arranging work have you seen that are effective? Where, when, and how?

As you reflect on your discussions about the preceding questions, ask yourself these questions:

1. **How does principle 11 challenge your assumptions about learning?**

2. **How does principle 11 challenge your assumptions about teaching?**

3. How does principle 11 challenge your assumptions about discipline?

4. How does principle 11 challenge your assumptions about assessment?

The whole is contained in every part.

17

Every Brain Is Uniquely Organized

Martha is a superb teacher in a middle school in the Bronx. Siegfried is an aspiring opera singer in Vienna. Teresa looks after her five brothers and sisters while both her parents are away, often for days at a time. Carol is on the school board but plans to run for the U.S. Senate. Bill and Jane work around the clock in their garage on the sculpture that they plan to enter in the annual artfest. James runs a factory in Cleveland that manufactures bicycles. About these people, the shaman in an African village and the tour guide in Mexico, and the other six billion or so who people the planet, we can say two things: They are all alike. And they are all different.

Although the brain/mind learning principles tend to be more or less generic in that they are true for everyone, each person remains unique. And the factors that make us the same are precisely those that allow us to be different. For example, we are all shaped by experience and yet we all have unique experiences that influence us uniquely.

Given our similarities and differences, we should expect to find patterns that we have in common, even while each one of us is unique. Scientists and artists have sought to identify common patterns in many ways, including the following:

- participation in various cultures

- personality and perceptual styles, beginning with specific factors such as extroversion and introversion as measured by the Myers-Briggs personality tests

- talents and intelligences, the most popular theory about which is currently Howard Gardner's multiple intelligences

- the interests, hobbies, occupations, and professions we share, irrespective of personality differences

This chapter introduces individual differences in various ways, then examines their implications for learning, teaching, and education generally.

Examining Individual Differences

Every brain is uniquely organized, so there are no two people exactly alike. However, there are overriding similarities such as those documented by these brain/mind learning principles. For example, principle 11 states that all people learn best in a low-threat, high-challenge environment. Yet what people perceive as threat or challenge varies. Some people like mountain climbing and hang gliding, whereas others are distinctly ill at ease with such activities.

There are many approaches to the art of assessing individual differences. One way is to build profiles through observation and a specific set of questions. We suggest that you begin by using an assessment tool to assess yourself and others whom you know well, then exploring the differences that it reveals. You might like to explore the work of Howard Gardner to see to what degrees your colleagues, your students, and you have the various intelligences.

We briefly describe four possible perceptual styles that you might like to explore in this manner. They are Geoffrey and Renate Caine's synthesis of many different approaches.

Adventurer

Change and variety, including a variety of sensory experiences, are very important to you. You are quick to anticipate what is going to happen. You live in a world of possibilities, and you are willing to look at things that are unique. You tend not to take authority too seriously. To you there is always another way, and if rules or people don't make sense to you, you ignore them and develop your own. You love sensation, variety, and fun, and often find yourself involved in several projects and ideas at the same time. The risk is that you lose a sense of orderliness and respect for other people's perspectives, and may not complete tasks.

Director

Big tasks and leadership are extremely important to you, and you like to have and give direction. You tend to make decisions quickly and stick to them. You want the facts before making any decision, but you tend to be impatient with detail and look for the big picture. It is important to you to understand what is happening and how things work. Words and sounds are very important to you, and you tend to take seriously what someone says. You are good at discerning when people do not mean what they say, and you do not like those people at all. You easily put pressure on others even if you hate being under pressure yourself. You may alienate people by seeming not to care about them or being too sharp or abrupt.

Evaluator

Order and system are very important to you. How things "look," either in the real world or in your mind, is also important. Your first impression of a person or place is based on what you see rather than on a conversation. You also care what other people think of you and how you look to them. You love events and things to be well ordered and to have a beginning, a middle, and an end. You are systematic and a good planner, and you like things to take place according to your plans. The result is that you have expectations about how things will turn out, and you can be inflexible and may find it difficult to adjust when something unexpected happens. You may also be overly critical, which can stop you from enjoying life as much as you could.

Nurturer

Being close to people is extremely important to you. And you love to touch, so working with your hands is also important. You have intense feelings of loyalty, and friends are central to your happiness. You need people around you, and you can become depressed and morose when alone. Because you care so much, you like to help others. You work hard for causes that you believe in. Your desire to work hard means that you can also be used by others because you are anxious to please them. You may end up giving too much, then feeling hurt and resentful. You tend to need details for reassurance and to get frustrated if you don't get adequate instructions. You prefer a lot of help and support to make sure you are doing things correctly.

 ### Activity 1: Exploring Personalities

Each of these personalities is likely to function differently from the others. Pool your experience and sense of how each would do the following:

- **How might each type downshift? Do some retreat and some attack? Do some hide and others take center stage?**

- **How might each relate to new people? Do some come close and others stay away? Do some act while others react?**

- What sources of sensory input are most important to each? Do some prefer sight, sound, touch? Do some like all sensory input equally?

- What decision and leadership styles would you expect from each? Would some leap in while others sit on the fence? Are there natural leaders and followers? Do some like detail while others begin with a big picture?

- Can you perceive differences in students along the lines revealed by these instruments?

- What are the implications for your work as an educator?

- To what extent might you have to change to communicate effectively with each type? How might you go about that sort of change?

Commentary

There is a great danger in overgeneralizing, and there is danger in relying too heavily on differences. We might label and pigeonhole people, and by so doing limit their and our capacity to grow. What instances of such labeling do you find going on in your workplace?

We might ignore the fact that some differences are context dependent, and so would not show up in a context different from the one in which we are used to dealing with people. What instances of losing sight of the context have happened to you?

 ### Activity 2: Making Differences Meaningful

It is important to appreciate people's unique approaches to creating meaning. Walking a mile in someone else's moccasins provides some excellent lessons. Following is a list of processes to explore:

- We suggest in chapter 16 that you keep a journal of your thoughts and reflections as you examine this book. **If you trust one another enough, exchange books and journals.** What do you notice about your colleagues?

- **Live someone else's life for a while—even in small ways.** Reduce your discretionary spending by 50 percent for one week (if you can). Exchange housekeeping roles with a person with whom you live for a week. Select a philosopher or psychologist who has a prescription for living and practice some aspect of that prescription diligently. Take a weekend course, but adopt a new name and background, and don't let anyone know you've done so. Record what happens.

- Select a culture that seems to be very different from yours but that is present in the place where you live and work. **Spend some time becoming familiar with that culture.** Examine critical questions from the perspective of that culture. Do those perspectives shed any light on your beliefs and assumptions?

- **Suspend judgment while listening to another.**

- **Be aware of how your predispositions, assumptions, or fatigue can influence the ways in which you listen to another.**

Challenge to Practice

Note that all the other principles shed light on principle 12:

- We all have unique purposes and meanings and therefore to some extent create unique maps of the world.

- As learning engages the entire physiology, and we each have unique physical equipment, we will each be unlike everyone else in the world in some respects.

- Learning is partly social, and as we each have unique clusters of friends and acquaintances and circumstances, our learnings will be unique in some respects.

Educators have a difficult task. We need to reach and teach all our students, yet they are different in so many ways. Our solution (developed at length in the rest of this book) is that educators should, among other things, seek to build community and to create complex projects and experiences. These approaches provide opportunities for various styles and preferences to find a place, while providing a framework that combines them all.

A Question to Explore as a Learner

What do principle 12 and the ideas in this chapter suggest for your own learning?

Questions to Explore as an Educator

How do we get a handle on the richly diverse array of talents and beliefs that are present in any classroom?

How do we capitalize on diversity?

Are we likely to find it easier to work with diversity in simple or complex environments? What do *simple* and *complex* mean to you?

How does one deal with individual differences without falling victim to inappropriate labeling and the imposition of false limitations or unrealistic expectations?

As you reflect on your discussions about the preceding questions, ask yourself these questions:

1. **How does principle 12 challenge your assumptions about learning?**

2. **How does principle 12 challenge your assumptions about teaching?**

3. **How does principle 12 challenge your assumptions about discipline?**

4. **How does principle 12 challenge your assumptions about assessment?**

PART 3

Making It Happen

The brain does the learning. Our job is to help it. It can record nonsense. It can also make sense. The conditions that we set up govern which of the two prevails.

We are now in a better position to grasp the overall shift in mental models that needs to take place. We need to shift education from an industrial age mental model attuned to the memorization of facts and skills to a mental model based on guided experience for meaningful learning.

From Industrial Model	**To Mental Model for Guided Experience**
Coercive discipline based on use of threat and power	Relaxed alertness: low threat and high challenge grounded in authentic community and relationship
Delivery of facts and skills	Orchestrated immersion in complex experience with meaningful content
Rote practice	Active processing of experience
Standardized tests	Standardized tests *plus* authentic assessment
An environment that supports these conditions	An environment that supports these conditions

Note that each model functions as a whole. The reason change is often so difficult and the results so mixed is that people seek to make small changes but fail to integrate them into a complete shift. The theory of practices and the nature of meaningful learning explored in part 3 show ways to shift toward profound learning and much higher standards.

Understanding these two mental models is also key to making much better use of all the other inservicing that you will receive, and will help you better know how to react to all the mandates you receive.

We Indians think of the Earth and the whole universe as a neverending circle, and in this circle man is just another animal. The buffalo and the coyote are our brothers, the birds, our cousins. Even the tiniest ant, even a louse, even the smallest flower you can find—they are all relatives.

—Jenny Leading Cloud

18

Reconceptualizing What We Want Students to Learn

When we ask the question "What do we want students to know?" the answer seems obvious. We might answer "math" or "scientific method" or "how to write effectively" or "the history of the United States." The problem is that statements such as these gloss over some very basic questions—specifically, what is meant by knowing?

What is actually being measured or assessed? The answers to these questions are not obvious, which is a source of much of the confusion that enmeshes education and discussions about ways to improve it. The brain/mind learning principles suggest that various types or levels of knowledge exist. If we concentrate on the wrong type of knowledge, we may actually lower standards rather than raise them.

Surface Knowledge: Decontextualized Facts and Basic Routines

The industrial delivery model of education tends to deal with the acquisition of surface knowledge—information and routines that are unrelated to student goals or deeper understanding. It is the stuff that is simply memorized by rote.

Those of us who visit classrooms, read textbooks, and listen to students see an educational system that has stripped much of the meaning from the curricula and the process of learning. If we hear the statement "Today we are going to learn about the steamboat" or "molecules" or *The Old Man and the Sea,*" we say to ourselves, "So what?" and wait to hear if our question is answered. Usually, it isn't. So we often hear students complain, "Why do I have to learn that?" It doesn't matter to students that the material may be important later on; for them it is useless because it isn't useful at that time.

The three of us speak of acquiring surface knowledge as "jumping through hoops" because it has little perceived value or real meaning for the learner. It is memorized for the test and then, almost invariably, forgotten. There are very few connections drawn between it and other knowledge, social and emotional issues, or other aspects of the learner's psyche. In the words of the great philosopher Alfred North Whitehead (1985), surface knowledge is "inert knowledge." Inert knowledge is that which is dry, lifeless, and has no point. It undermines the sense of possibility that real knowing ignites. Whitehead suggests that the greatest threat to education is inert knowledge. He is also reputed to have said that "knowledge doesn't keep any better than fish." Perhaps we have too many dead fish in our educational process.

➤ *Activity 1: Discovering Surface Knowledge*

Respond to the following questions:

When have you had to acquire only surface knowledge?

How did you feel?

Do you ever teach only surface knowledge?

Who or what influences you to teach it?

Technical, or Scholastic, Knowledge

A more complex level of learning involves grasping underlying concepts intellectually. The distinction between facts and concepts is critical. In the industrial model, we focus on topics to be covered. The guided-experience model calls for teaching for meaning using concepts (see chapter 9). A fact is a bit of information that can be remembered. A concept is essentially an organizing idea—it shows how various facts are connected. It functions somewhat as a map that puts facts in relation to each other. The crucial result is that a concept allows us to connect facts in appropriate ways, even when we are just seeing the facts for the first time. Thus, a concept is a higher-order pattern than a fact.

When we focus on the names of kings, queens, presidents, and dates of reigns or years in office, we teach surface knowledge. When we make some attempt to teach an understanding of what a king or queen or president is, we teach a concept. The following questions reflect a stab at deeper understanding. What is a monarch? What is royalty? How is a president of a republic different from a monarch? In what ways are they similar?

Now, it is fairly easy to teach these ideas as though they were just facts; we simply provide a list of attributes for students to remember. We might include, for example, that a president must be elected whereas a king or queen inherits the title and responsibilities. Whether or not students grasp the concepts themselves depends on what you allow them to do with questions and problems you introduce. For instance, are there counterexamples that show that some presidents are appointed and not elected, or that show people becoming monarchs without inheriting the title? Alternatively, we might present some apparently unrelated scenarios and ask how the people in them are like monarchs or presidents. Examples include heads of families, members of the federal reserve, chief executive officers of corporations. In essence, seeing examples and counterexamples, comparing similarities and differences, noting essential characteristics, and so on can unlock key aspects of a concept.

Students can master some routines and procedures using this process as well. In literature, for example, students can be introduced to the notions of a plot, characters, setting, and dramatic tension, then find them in a novel or play or ongoing political saga.

 ### *Activity 2: Discovering Concepts in Curriculum*

Respond to the following questions:

Select an aspect of the curriculum with which you are involved. What are the critical concepts?

Are they taught as facts or as concepts?

How do you know?

Commentary

Concept learning is more complex than memorization. A learner has to be able to organize and solve problems with the material. Thus, learners master some routes and routines that can be very useful. Examples include strategies for solving equations, analyzing the plot of a novel, examining the causes of historical events, carrying out experiments in a laboratory, and so on. When educators talk about teaching for understanding, they tend to mean teaching for technical or scholastic knowledge. While it is absolutely critical for making sense of information and for solving hypothetical problems, technical and scholastic knowledge is also limited.

Dynamical knowledge is different from technical knowledge because it is really useful. We can describe it as being like a living map. It involves a quality of understanding that is so real and rich that a person can use the concepts and ideas naturally in the course of everyday living. For the concepts to be used in this way, the students must have internalized the "learnings," the knowledge, in such a way that their perceptions of the world have changed.

A great source of examples is found with people who have a consuming interest, such as the photographer who sees every event in terms of light, shade, and symbols; the developer who sees all green areas in terms of real estate; the politician who sees every new acquaintance as a potential vote; the gardener who looks at a statue or house in terms of its impact on the landscape; the musician who hears everything in terms of discord and harmony. They use their professional knowledge to make sense of their world. Something rather special has happened: concepts have come alive in the minds of people; these concepts now shape perception. There is now a difference in the way that these people spontaneously and naturally perceive and interpret the world.

 ### Activity 3: Exploring Conceptual Learning

Respond to the following questions:

Identify instances when you have internalized concepts to the point where they have naturally become incorporated in your life and shape your reactions. We mention some examples in the preceding paragraphs.

Elaborate on some of these examples in your discussion. What is the texture or quality of the difference between concepts intellectually understood and concepts that are part and parcel of how you perceive your world?

Commentary

Differences show up readily in the use of analogy and metaphor, as when a student can look at the president, for instance, and say spontaneously (and, perhaps, satirically) "their royal highnesses, the president and spouse." Taking the issue of monarchs and presidents further, this natural understanding shows up if a student can use the concepts in the course of everyday events on campus. Imagine a student article or cartoon in which the principal is dressed up in robes and the teachers are kneeling at his or her feet.

Here you have evidence of some deep understanding. The key here is the natural use of these analogies and metaphors, not just their planned use in papers and portfolios.

We must caution you here: We have been writing as though things were black and white—either people fully understand something or they don't. Things are not that clear-cut. There are degrees of "getting it" and degrees of expertise. For example, we can learn more and more about computers or politics. There is always more to learn, and understanding can always be improved. But there is a quality to real understanding that is very different from rote learning or intellectual understanding. And the brain functions differently in developing this quality, which is what the brain/mind principles demonstrate.

Creating Dynamical Knowledge

We have been distinguishing among surface, technical/scholastic, and dynamical knowledge. All three types of knowledge are important. Sometimes students need to memorize facts and procedures. And grasping underlying concepts in any subject is vital. However, the knowledge that is ultimately most practical, useful, and powerful is dynamical knowledge. Our goal, therefore, is to support educators in helping their students acquire dynamical knowledge. Dynamical knowledge is genuinely meaningful to the learner. When students have grasped something at this level, then much more of the brain—including the emotions, the senses, and the body—has been engaged in a focused and synthesized way. The quality of the knowledge and understanding is different from surface or technical, scholastic knowledge. This quality is one reason for the strong trend in recent years away from the industrial model of education toward one based on guided experience.

The process of learning to this depth is somewhat like a chemical reaction, with dynamical knowledge as the product. It is the way knowledge interacts with our experience that allows us to build meaningful ideas and values. The brain/mind learning principles indicate that there are two aspects of meaning that *must* be integrated if dynamical knowledge is to occur. We call those two aspects *felt meaning* and *deep meaning.*

227

Felt Meaning: What Really Makes Sense

In *Making Connections: Teaching and the Human Brain,* we define *felt meaning* (a term borrowed from Gendlin 1962) as "an unarticulated sense of relationship that culminates with the aha of insight."

The "Aha!" of Insight

We all know what it is like to have a flash of insight or understanding, when things suddenly come together and make sense.

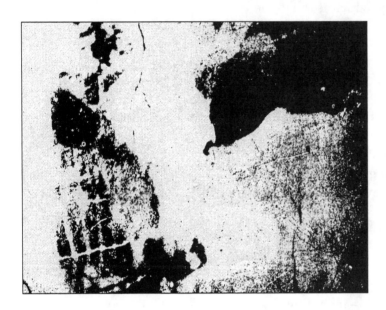

 Activity 4: Exploring Sudden Insights

Look at the pictures. What do you see? (The answer is at the end of the chapter.)

Commentary

This exercise is basically one in visual perception, but the same sudden insight that occurs when you see what the picture really is happens with all our other senses. There is a coming together of parts in a way that "fits." We might experience an "aha" when a metaphor in a poem suddenly makes sense. We might have an "aha" when we master a bit of software, see the way to solve a financial problem, finally understand what the word *variable* means in math, or understand an aspect of the relationship between Congress and the White House.

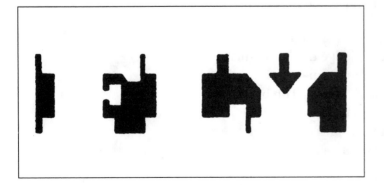

A frequently remarked-on experience is the sense of relief and energy that often accompanies this type of insight. Sometimes the sensation is very slight. Other insights evoke emotions ranging from awe to an almost mystical sense of oneness to joy and delight.

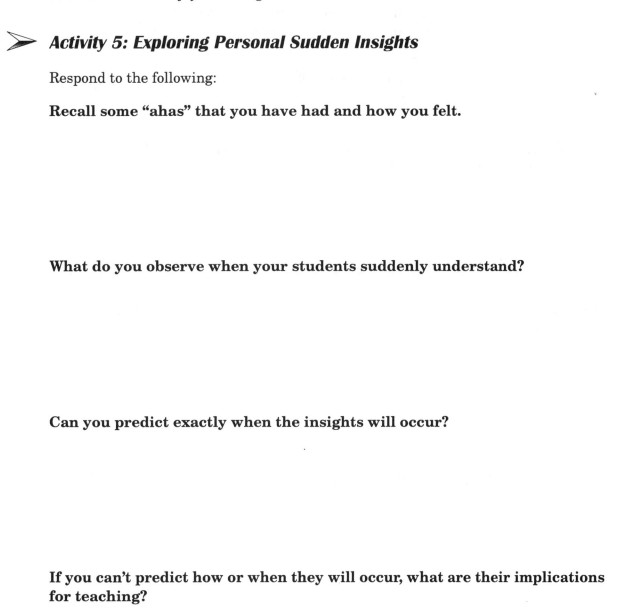

➤ *Activity 5: Exploring Personal Sudden Insights*

Respond to the following:

Recall some "ahas" that you have had and how you felt.

What do you observe when your students suddenly understand?

Can you predict exactly when the insights will occur?

If you can't predict how or when they will occur, what are their implications for teaching?

A Sense of Relationship

When we are thinking about any subject area or skill, there is more than the "aha" moment, which is often just the tip of the iceberg. There is a sense of relationship—of feeling at home in the waters of the subject, as it were. The following questions will help you elicit this feeling.

➤ ## *Activity 6: Exploring Relationships to Learning*

Respond to the following:

Think of a topic that you love and another that you strongly dislike. Compare the ways that you feel about the two of them.

What was it like in the beginning, when you just had to remember a few facts that did not mean much?

How was that different from your current knowledge?

How would you describe the difference between knowing something in theory and "really" knowing it?

The Sources of Felt Meaning

One reason for using *felt* in this context is that there is much more than merely linguistic or "cognitive" functioning. There is a physical recognition that something has been learned.

In fact felt meaning engages multiple brain/mind systems working synergistically. There are sensory, emotional, and physiological components to meaning. You will find attention and peripheral perception, multiple levels of sensory input, focused attention and unconscious processing, the interrelations of parts and wholes, a much greater capacity to have insights when not feeling threatened or helpless, unique ways of approaching the same problem, a significant flow and range of emotional involvement, and more.

To repeat, our goal in education is to have students "see" what a subject is all about. We want them to have a felt meaning for an idea or skill, because then we know that they are on their way to real knowledge and genuine mastery. However, developing this sense of relationship and insight takes time. It can be influenced, but not controlled or predicted. In fact, it involves a type of teaching that takes us beyond the traditional delivery model, and we consider this method in more detail in the next chapter.

Deep Meanings: The Driving Force

Deep meanings are at the heart of intrinsic motivation, because they are the sum of what is important to us. They are the values, purposes, assumptions, convictions, and passions that drive us. They are particularly important in education for two reasons. First, they are key to learning anything at all. Second, they act as "attractors" around which learning is organized. They are the forces that shape the maps that we create of how the world works.

Deep meanings connect *what* is learned to *why* it is important to the learner. The student has a purpose beyond the knowing that links the content and the learning process to the learner in a personal and integral way.

Motivation

Every human mind harbors complex values and beliefs that govern what is perceived to be important. Abraham Maslow (1968), for instance, suggested that every human being has a hierarchy of motives and needs. And George Kelly believed that everyone is different and that we all combine ideas in our own way. He showed that we can identify some of the individual "constructs" of each person, constructs that reveal what is and is not important to that person.

Ideas and values can become more important to us than life itself. Think of the concepts freedom, love, and right and wrong, all of which provide for us the very purpose for living. One of the great joys of teaching is to share what is meaningful to us in ways that help students glimpse the excitement, usefulness, and relevance of that knowledge to their own lives.

Deep meanings bring purpose to experience. They are extremely powerful in hindering or driving a person. In fact, deep meanings actually guide the selection of many of the experiences that we have, the way those experiences are perceived, and the value we place on them. Hence, we must pay attention to the deep meanings of our students.

 ### *Activity 7: Exploring Deep Meaning*

Respond to the following:

Think about some activity that you have felt driven to do, or some subject or skill that you have had a strong urge to learn and master. Why did you feel so strongly?

What was (or would be) needed to stop you from pursuing that interest?

Did your interest or passion keep you going when times were tough or you had to overcome difficulties?

Did you put time into the subject or skill even when you "should" have been doing something else?

Commentary

Deep meanings have a fundamental role in the shape and structure of the Self. Indeed, they also set up the barriers to what a person can or will learn. They provide direction and energy for what actually becomes real knowledge. They are always operative. At a minimum they must be acknowledged. It is because meaningfulness is so profoundly dependent on deep meanings that good teaching does all that it can to engage and capitalize on what students find to be really important and interesting. A word of caution is needed, however. Deep meanings offer immense opportunity—and pose significant problems—for educators. On the one hand deep meanings for students are crucial aspects of high challenge, so they need to be engaged. On the other hand, the values that students have (and that some teachers have) may be founded on profound bigotry and prejudice. They may be totally contrary to what we are setting out to teach. Moreover, we interpret students' values and purposes—their deep meanings—through our own filters.

It is not our task here to prescribe what ought to be taught. However, in the chapters that follow we deal with how to teach for real meaning.

Assessment for the Guided-Experience Model

If we are teaching for dynamical knowledge, we need to know how to assess it and what to look for. The key to demonstrating the acquisition of dynamical knowledge is real-world performance. For example, to what extent would students who have "learned to analyze the causes of war" be able to analyze the nature of gang conflict and urban warfare? Or respond differently from the way they currently respond to conflict in their own class, school, or society?

Following are some indicators of the acquisition of dynamical knowledge:

- The ability to use the language of the discipline or subject in complex situations and in social interaction

- The ability to perform appropriately in unanticipated situations

- The ability to use skills and concepts of any discipline or subject to solve problems outside the classroom

- The ability to show, explain, or teach the idea or skill to another person who has a real need to know

- The ability to examine consciously and deliberately their performance in various contexts and to appreciate their own strengths and weaknesses

Practical Implications for Basic Issues

The distinctions that we examine are very powerful because they influence many of the basic issues that concern us.

Memorization

We have suggested that, most of the time, it is inappropriate to teach just for memorization. Yet we all want students to remember facts. What the research shows is that students remember many, many facts naturally and easily if we teach for meaning.

Have you ever observed first- and second-graders studying dinosaurs? The children learn incredibly difficult names, habitats, and identifying characteristics. It seems that the more they learn, the more they want to know. Is it the knowledge about dinosaurs itself that creates this excitement, or could it be the idea of dinosaur?

The idea of huge creatures stimulates an imaginary world inside the child that just keeps going. Students draw pictures, play make-believe with small model dinosaurs, hug stuffed replicas, and re-create an imaginary existence. By mediating the world of dinosaur information and the imaginative world of the child, you can observe the relationship of knowledge and meaning.

You can add more and more "facts" as long as you keep alive the "idea" of dinosaurs on which children can anchor memory. Once the idea is squelched, however, the facts tend to lose their fascination. And when meaning is lost, memory becomes a burden. Even if the testing that we use tests for memorization, we should still teach for deep meaning because the best way to have students memorize facts is to teach for meaning.

Standards and Assessment

The call in many countries is for higher standards. But determining whether standards have been met requires that we know how to assess what students know. Because the industrial mental model guides most assessment, such assessment boils down to testing for facts. The problem is that testing for facts causes us to organize all our time teaching for memorization. So we end up teaching much less effectively.

If we really want to teach for meaning, we have to have modes of assessment that support us in teaching for meaning. But because standardized tests are so important to the community, we also need students to be able to perform well on them.

How can we solve the problem? Whether we like it or not, standardized tests will not go away. Our task as educators is to avoid being intimidated or dominated by them. The guided-experience model calls for adding authentic assessment because this type of assessment supports teaching for meaning. As we *master* authentic assessment, we need to learn how to embed the material that is found on standardized tests in our teaching, and learn ways simply to include some standardized testing in what we do. Results improve because students learn more and perform better when we teach for meaning—and this improved performance also shows up on standardized tests. It is for these reasons that authentic assessment becomes important as the primary mode of assessment.

Discipline

One of the greatest problems facing education is discipline in schools. Yet the problem is partly of our own making. Many discipline problems occur because children are not engaged. Children of all ages are much more likely to be on task and engaged when they are involved in something meaningful. When we teach for real meaning, that in itself helps to solve our discipline problems. We need to explore the art and practice of teaching for meaning. Teaching for real meaning, we should add, is extraordinarily exhilarating but is as difficult to do well as any task in any other profession in the known world. Moreover, like any complex profession, the art and skill must be developed over time. Teaching for meaning is not just about accumulating more instructional strategies or techniques for classroom management.

Our solution, which we present in the first two parts of this book, begins with helping educators gain a felt meaning for what learning is all about. The next two chapters set in motion the process for systematically improving instruction and administration. The first step is to translate the brain/mind learning principles and the goal of teaching for dynamical knowledge into a theory of instructional practice.

An Added Caution

Even when we use concepts to teach for meaning, we must make certain that facts and skills are adequately consolidated in students' minds. In the guided-experience mental model, such consolidation becomes a critical teaching skill. We must have internalized the standards and gently but continually guide student learning so that students understand the highest standards and meet them without teachers having to resort to coercion or power, such as using rewards and punishments.

Note: The first image in the felt meaning exercise is of a cow; the second spells the word *fly*.

19

Reconceptualizing Teaching: A Theory of Practice

When we apply the brain/mind principles, we see why experience is the most effective teacher. It is experience that engages the entire body and mind; it is experience that triggers emotions; it is experience through which we perceive the whole as well as the parts; it is experience that provides us with the opportunities to be engaged and challenged; it is experience through which our complex interactions result in rich social relationships; it is experience through which we are exposed to meaningful contexts; and so on.

Examine the places where you work—in most cases, schools.

> ## *Activity 1: Examining the Place You Work*

Given what you've learned from examining the brain/mind learning principles, how do we explain the following?

45- to 55-minute time segments for specific subjects

curriculum framed around a chronological year

divisions by age into grades

10, 20, or 30 students in a class

multiple-choice tests

an emphasis on maintaining discipline as the foundation for teaching

an emphasis on identifying, then seeking to individually remediate a large number of ostensible "learning deficits"

a primary emphasis on phonics in reading

waiting until middle or high school to teach new languages

cutting back on the arts

a preponderance of teacher talk

Commentary

Other small and large issues permeate every corner of the education world. They involve standards, including the call for world-class standards for every child; multiculturalism; methods of testing and assessment; safety and discipline in schools; retention; differences between the have and the have nots; the proper role of technology in education; effective teacher training; and more.

Every one of these issues is about practice. How should we approach them?

A Theory of Practice

The brain/mind principles lead to some very strong implications about the essential nature of good teaching. More specifically, the Caines show in *Making Connections* that there are three interactive elements that stand out as being indispensable for using guided experience to teach for meaning:

- relaxed alertness as an optimal state of mind

- the orchestrated immersion of the learner in complex experiences in which curriculum is embedded

- the active processing of the experience so that the learners create the potential meanings that are there

The three interactive elements look like the diagram. By using these three elements, we have a way to integrate the twelve brain/mind learning principles to better allow us to think about teaching and administering educational environments. The three elements also become a more convenient frame of reference for assessing and implementing new techniques and strategies.

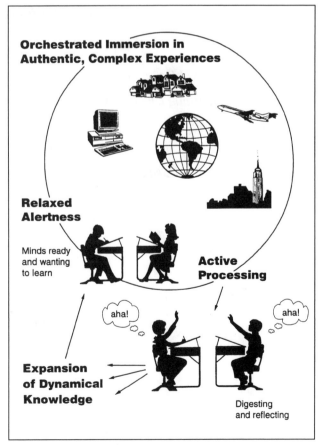

241

Relaxed Alertness as an Optimal State of Mind

We know that complex learning is enhanced by challenge and inhibited by threat. However, it is important to understand the nuances of the phrases *low threat* and *high challenge*. We do *not* mean that students should never feel fear or anxiety, as both are natural aspects of life. Low threat means that, in general, students do not feel helpless. That is, they have a good sense of self-efficacy or a realistic confidence in their ability to succeed. And high challenge does not mean that we inevitably ask students to do very complex things. High challenge is the extent to which they are personally engaged; that is, it refers to their wanting to do complex things in the course of their search for meaning.

In short, our job is to create conditions under which students feel safe, confident, welcome, and intrinsically motivated. The first step in creating those conditions is to build or grow a real learning community.

Basic Elements of a Learning Community

The objective of brain-compatible instruction is for the school to become a learning community where there is respect for all, a degree of orderliness, and taken-for-granted behaviors. One reason we emphasize the group process is it begins to create this overall climate, which is essential for individual teachers to feel relaxed alertness.

Indicators and Questions: A Checklist of Learning Community Factors

❑ Is the temperature comfortable?

❑ Does the setting, including architecture and layout, support group work and private study?

❑ Is the environment lighthearted or depressing? What messages does it send to children and adults?

❏ How much street noise do students hear? What sorts of distraction does the intercom system create?

❏ Is there artwork and other decoration around the room? Does it include posters of great works of art? Are students given the message that competence and quality are recognized and endorsed?

❏ What sort of group atmosphere is emerging?

❏ Are students helping one another with projects and concepts?

❏ Is there a way to introduce interesting places and changes in the physical environment? Is it done?

❏ Is technology used to enhance or diminish the environment? How can you tell?

❏ Do teachers, administrators, and staff support one another? Are students aware of the actual organizational atmosphere?

❏ Is there any connection between course content (such as economics) and other school activities (such as fund-raising)?

❏ Do the school priorities reflect, in action, ostensible curriculum priorities? What value is placed on sports, socials, local politics, and educational goals?

❏ Is school happening inside and outside the classroom?

Establishing Intrinsic Motivation in Students

When students are intrinsically motivated they take charge of much of their learning. Even if test results are below expectations for a while, when you have evidence of self-directed and self-energized activity related to course content, your students are open to and actively engaged in meaningful learning. Note that students can be on task in many different ways. For example, voluntarily returning to a project or problem is often much more of an indicator of ultimate success than dutifully doing busy work for a fixed length of time.

Indicators and Questions: A Checklist of Intrinsic Motivation Factors

❏ Is there clear evidence of student involvement, creativity, and enjoyment?

❏ Are there many different moods, including playfulness and serious thought?

❏ Are students asking questions or making observations that link content to life?

❏ Are their personal life themes, metaphors, interests, and dreams being engaged? For example, do students introduce course content into personal discussions and play in the class?

❏ What signs of continuing motivation or student interest express themselves above and beyond the dictates of the class?

❏ Do students persevere with projects or return to them without being reminded?

❏ Are there any signs of positive collaboration? Does the collaboration continue after the lesson and after school?

❏ Are students dealing appropriately with dissonance? For example, do they persevere to overcome difficulties in understanding or communication, or do they just give up at the first signs of difficulty?

❏ Do students suggest relevant projects of their own?

Orchestrated Immersion in Complex Experience

Even though traditional education tends to leave life out, life is still going on. As you examined the brain/mind learning principles, you and the other members of your group may have had many suggestions regarding how to create experiences. Possibilities range from using projects and stories to enhancing the peripheral environment and creating conditions for complex social interactions.

➤ *Activity 2: Exploring Immersion*

Respond to the following:

- **Do students interact with one another in the classroom in multiple ways?**

- **Do you see a range of emotions in these interactions?**

- **What aspects of the outside world come into the classroom?**

- **What other evidence of lived experience do you see? For instance, to what extent do students venture into the outside world as part of their coursework?**

Our task as educators is to capitalize on students' life experiences and help them use their entire experience to support learning. We need to guide learning so that the crucial aspects of the curriculum, ideas, and skills, are included in ongoing lived experience. That is what we mean by orchestrating the immersion of the learner in complex experience in which curriculum is embedded.

Many strategies and procedures that have been developed in recent years are geared toward orchestrated immersion. They range from packaged materials to project-based learning. The challenge is always to do more than simply present information in disguise. Learning how to meet this challenge will be one of the most important issues for you to explore as you take part in the expanded Mindshifts process described in chapter 20.

The Active Processing of Experience

The brain/mind does not simply sit there inactive, like a storm drain that allows water to flow through. The brain/mind learning principles show us that we constantly monitor our experience as we form and test the maps that help us make sense of life. The locale system, for instance, checks out anything new to make sense of it. Human beings have the capacity to react instantly to a threatening stimulus. And when we say that parts and wholes are processed simultaneously, we mean that each is being checked against the other: Is a specific event a significant part of the plot? How does what she said fit into what I thought our relationship was all about? Doesn't this fork in the road seem out of place?

Active processing is the learner's consolidation and internalization of information and procedures in ways that are personally meaningful and conceptually coherent. Active processing, then, is the key to perceiving patterns and making sense of experience.

Such processing is so innate that it is present in every field and area of expertise. Experts and professionals always process experience: lawyers ask critical questions; doctors rely on keen observation to diagnose; architects relate form to function; therapists look and listen for hidden meanings; coaches monitor skill, performance, and attitude.

The problem comes with what Ellen Langer (1989) called "premature cognitive commitments." It is very easy to be happy with the patterns that we already see and totally oblivious to what else is happening. But if we rely only on patterns we have developed alone, we may have an experience without learning anything new from it. A fundamental task of the educator, after orchestrating experience for students, is to guide and support them in actively processing that experience so they discover and create new patterns and meanings. You will find that many subjects in the curriculum provide tools for processing experience. They include critical thinking, testing of hypotheses, reflective journaling, in-depth observation, a search for central metaphors, and so on.

The Theory of Brain-Based Learning and Teaching at Work

One way to see the theory at work is to see how we have learned in situations outside school.

 ## Activity 3: Exploring Hobbies

Think of any skill or subject area in which you have become really proficient, so proficient that you can actually perform it successfully. A hobby is one good example. You might want to revisit the experience you used in chapter 14.

Relaxed Alertness

Reflect on your attitudes, motives, interests—your ongoing state of mind as you developed proficiency. To what extent do you have a personal interest in this area? Do you choose to think about it and work on it in your own time?

To what extent has your success depended on a feeling or belief that you could be at least moderately proficient?

Did you ever feel safe enough to risk making mistakes? Have there been moments or longer times of confusion, uncertainty, and ambiguity? Would you expect to have such moments?

Have you ever been forced to rethink what you were doing by coming face to face with an idea that was wrong or a procedure that no longer worked? Was that dissonant experience valuable?

Orchestrated Immersion in Complex Experience

As you think about the subject or skill, you will see that you have actually engaged in a wide variety of activities and experiences that involve your field of interest. Some were planned; others, happenstance.

Has your interest been played out in a variety of physical contexts (in a club, at home, outdoors)?

Have you had planned and accidental discussions relating to it?

Have those discussions included peers, those older or younger, and experts of all types?

Has it been mentioned in the media, ranging from straight news to background settings in movies?

Has your interest demanded a variety of skills (ranging from writing or communicating to measuring and searching for significant patterns)?

Have you had some direct instruction?

Active Processing of Experience

Have you examined your own performance and results?

Have you sought feedback and advice from others?

Have you compared your work with that of others?

Have you tested concepts and procedures, perhaps pushing the boundary of what is allowed?

Have you found yourself engaged in some research for facts, information, relevant history?

Have others helped you with your understanding and development, perhaps with questions or suggestions?

To what extent do you seek assistance to help you improve or learn more?

Review

Look back at the introduction to part 3 and the distinction we make between the industrial model and the emerging model based on guided experience. You will see that the new model must work as a whole to be effective. With that in mind, we are now in a position to redefine the Mindshifts process and to focus more specifically on practice and skill development.

20

Ongoing Professional Development and the Renewal of Process

Although in this book we refer to the need to raise standards, we make almost no reference to skill development. Skill development and higher standards must be based on a solid foundation, and our concern has been to develop that foundation. We have done so by supporting you in identifying a mental model of how people learn that is grounded in the best theory of learning available, then supporting you in developing that mental model.

Meaningful learning, both of students and staff, also depends upon the existence of a really powerful community that incorporates rapport and trust, and provides everyone with opportunities to take risks and grow. One goal of the Mindshifts process has been to generate that sort of community. Also, professional and skill development is most effective when learning is constant and natural, which means that at all costs, you must maintain a reflective process. Such a process takes time to develop and become second nature, so we stress the creation of a process culture. Finally, as you have worked through the process, you have been developing your skills, for instance, as you explored the questions at the end of each chapter on the brain/mind principles. Now we turn to skill development more directly, but still within the framework of a reflective process.

Skill Development

Any profession requires many skills, and there are degrees of competence in and mastery of those skills. Once you have a sense of community, for instance, it is still important to consider ways to resolve conflict and to listen actively. Indeed, all the issues with which we begin this book remain. Do this activity from chapter 1 again:

To which of the following issues are you being exposed?

❑ authentic assessment

❑ whole language

❑ thematic instruction

❑ integrated curriculum

❑ block scheduling

❑ multiage grouping

❑ constructivism

❑ multiculturalism

❑ accountability

❑ peer coaching

❑ changing state and district mandates

❑ authentic experience

❑ reading recovery

❑ multimedia and computers

❑ cooperative learning

❑ site-based management

❑ action research

❑ full inclusion

❑ multiple intelligences

❑ changes in class size

❑ phonics-based programs

❑ standards and standardized tests

List other issues that arise or strategies and processes that are being introduced in some way into your professional environment.

- **Which of these make more sense to you now?**

- **Which make less sense?**

- **How do they fit into your new theory of effective teaching practices?**

- **To what extent and in what ways are they brain based?**

- **Within the list is a wealth of possibility for becoming more proficient. But how on earth do we do it all? How do we select? How do we integrate what we are exploring? How do we know what to work on? How do we work on it best?**

Personal Development

A parallel aspect of skill development is personal growth. In fact, we grow naturally as we change mental models because we change something about ourselves. The larger point is that to really master these skills, we have to have certain qualities. For example, let's say that building a sense of community is important to you. Strategies and an appropriate mental model help, but you also need to enjoy building relationships with your students. Without a sense of and desire for relationship, deep community—if it occurs at all—will happen despite you, not because of you. We suggest you read *Unleashing the Power of Perceptual Change* (Caine and Caine 1997d) to develop a clear perspective of the sorts of personal qualities that we believe need to emerge.

Renewal of Process

The process that will sustain you in your work has the same overall structure as the one described in chapter 5 but differs significantly in its focus. This focus is now more on skill development.

Your meetings will have the same three general phases as before:

Phase 1: Ordered Sharing

The ordered sharing sets the tone and creates the essential environment. We strongly advise that, for your core material, you return to the principles of connectedness on a regular basis because they will help you develop the qualities you need for complex instruction. This phase should be brief but included in each meeting; it is essential.

Phase 2: Analytical and Reflective Session

This session replaces the large middle block of the initial Mindshifts process. You no longer simply focus on the brain/mind principles. Rather, you explore specific issues and strategies, including any of those listed early in this chapter. The goal is to relate the new strategies to the theory of learning and practice.

This subprocess is illustrated in the diagram as a triangle. In this part of the group process, you move around the triangle, looking at the three elements: unpack the idea or strategy, relate the idea or strategy to the brain/mind learning principles and the theory of practice, and reflect on what the idea or strategy means for you personally.

Strategy

Ways Stategy Fits

What Stategy Means

- Strategy (for example, cooperative learning)

- Ways strategy fits the principles and theory

- What the appropriate strategy means for you personally

For example, if you were examining cooperative learning, this second phase of the process might work as follows:

1. Analyze the Strategy

Spend time clarifying the elements of cooperative learning using at least one person's version and written materials. Do you all agree on what basic terms mean? Are there other versions? What, specifically, does the group recommend to develop cooperative learning? In what ways does it change in each of several different contexts? Whom does it benefit?

Are there different versions of cooperative learning? What are the various roles involved in a cooperative learning structure? When and in what circumstances should group size change? Who determines membership?

2. Examine the Strategy in Terms of the Learning Theory

For any strategy, ask at least two questions:

1. To what extent and in what ways is it compatible or incompatible with or explained by the brain/mind learning principles?

2. How does the strategy match the theory of practice?

For example, cooperative learning seems compatible with principle 2, the brain/mind is social, and people do make meanings collectively. However, we also know that each brain is uniquely organized, so we know that cooperative learning will be perceived differently by different learners. Cooperative learning supports the creation of community in the classroom and can be valuable in developing relaxed alertness. However, if we don't deal with issues of status and control of the group, some people will end up feeling more helpless. For example, if you watch the groups carefully, you will notice that some students don't give others access to materials. The left-out students are often ignored; others perceive them as being unable to contribute. If, however, the tasks are designed to require problem solving and stress multiple possibilities and a variety of talents, then those student who are usually left out are more likely to be included; cooperative learning will be more consistent with all the principles.

3. Examine What It All Means for You

This phase is crucial because it is the point at which you begin to personalize the issues and explore your own strengths and weaknesses. Cooperative learning, for example, is intended to help you build a learning community. However, as you will have seen by now, community is not just the product of actions and strategies. It also depends on our capacity to build authentic relationships with people. Key to your success is your ability to build authentic relationships with your students, which involves your qualities as a person. A person who uses cooperative learning to disguise a form of discipline will have very different results from one who has an intrinsic appreciation for relationship.

Phase 3: Focusing on Your Path

In this final phase of the group process you consolidate what you have learned from the session and use it to decide what you will be working on in the coming weeks (or months). You may work on developing specific skills such as storytelling or asking probing questions, general skills such as creating community and using context more effectively, or personal development skills such as developing expertise or being patient.

The purpose is for you to take a few minutes to reflect on your chosen area of growth, then to use ordered sharing to let the group know what you have learned from the session and what you intend to work on. As your purposes become clear, you will find that you develop some very powerful change strategies. Peer coaching develops as you find a colleague or two working on the same area and decide to support one another during the week by keeping in touch to discuss progress. Action research is identifying something important to you, then systematically researching it in terms of your professional experience and understanding of brain-based learning. Many such strategies are available and we do not intend to endorse one over another by mentioning them here. The key is for you to choose and use a strategy in a way that is appropriate for you. You might even like to test the strategy in the reflective session as you would any other process or strategy.

Group Membership and Other Details

We have found that when the group shifts from dealing with learning to dealing with skill development like this, it often changes the membership. At this point, it might be appropriate to be in a group with others who are doing similar work, such as teachers with teachers, administrators with administrators. You will also want to have one or two other people in the group who are likely to share a specific interest such as subject matter or grade level. However, we strongly suggest that you continue to vary the membership by including people who have various interests and teachers of various grade levels. Such diversity will provide a richness and variety of exposure that is invaluable. Remember that membership is voluntary.

Leadership

Leadership is a delicate question here. Some natural leaders might be skilled and can be invaluable. However, they may often have a strong tendency to "teach" other members rather than support them in their learning. The group itself must decide how to handle leadership. Conflict resolution and active listening skills become crucial at this point.

Routines

In general, sustain the routines, procedures, and process principles outlined in chapters 3 and 4.

There Is Always More

The temptation to believe that there is a "there," an end to achieve, can be very strong. We close with a response from Ellen Giffin, one of the teachers with whom we have worked closely for several years. An interviewer once asked her, "What advice would you give other teachers?" She replied, "Start slowly, one step at a time. I know that I'm still taking those one steps at a time and I think that the biggest thing to know is that there's always more . . . I'm never going to have [a moment when I can say] 'Okay, my room is finished . . . this is brain-based learning . . . come on in.' It's not like that. It's just a growing process. You grow with the kids . . . and you change . . . Be kind to yourself. When you do hit something to celebrate, make sure to take the time to stop and celebrate and realize, 'Oh, I did that.'"

In fact, a crucial underlying aspect of this approach is that it is accompanied by continuous personal growth. You will find that mastering skills and developing new mental models all depend on the emergence of additional personal qualities in us as human beings. Brain-compatible learning is a process. You always get better and discover more about yourself. Most of all, you become comfortable with the fact that there is always more.

Bibliography

Allport, S. 1986. *Explorer of the Black Box: The Search for the Cellular Basis of Memory.* New York: W. W. Norton.

Belenky, M. F., B. M. Clinchy, N. R. Goldberger, and J. M. Tarule. 1986. *Women's Ways of Knowing.* New York: Basic.

Blum, D. 1997. *Sex on the Brain: The Biological Differences between Men and Women.* New York: Viking.

Caine, G., and R. N. Caine. 1997. *MindShifts.* Video. Tucson, Ariz.: Zephyr Press.

Caine, R. N., and G. Caine. 1997a. *Education on the Edge of Possibility.* Alexandria, Va.: ASCD.

———. 1994. *Making Connections: Teaching and the Human Brain.* Menlo Park, Calif.: Addison Wesley.

———. 1997b. *Teaching and the Human Brain.* Video. Tucson, Ariz.: Zephyr Press.

———. 1997c. *Unleashing the Power of Perceptual Change: The Potential of Brain-Based Teaching.* Alexandria, Va.: ASCD.

Capra, F. 1996. *The Web of Life.* New York: Anchor.

Cole, K. C. 1998. "Why the Arts Are Important to Science." *Los Angeles Times* August 13: B1.

Crowell, S., R. N. Caine, and G. Caine. 1997. *The Re-Enchantment of Learning: A Manual for Teacher Renewal and Classroom Reformation.* Tucson, Ariz.: Zephyr Press.

Csikszentmihalyi, M. 1990. *Flow: The Psychology of Optimal Experience.* New York: Harper Perennial.

Damasio, A. R. 1994. *Descartes' Error: Emotion, Reason, and the Human Brain.* New York: Avon.

Darling, D. 1996. *Zen Physics.* New York: HarperCollins.

Deci, E. L, and R. M. Ryan. 1987. *The Psychology of Self-Determination.* Lexington, Mass.: D. C. Heath.

Diamond, M., and J. Hopson. 1998. *Magic Trees of the Mind: How to Nurture Your Child's Intelligence, Creativity, and Healthy Emotion.* New York: Penguin, Putnam.

Diamond, M. C., D. Krech, and M. R. Rosenzweig. 1964. "The Effects of an Enriched Environment on the Histology of the Rat Cerebrum Cortex." *J. Comp. Neurol.* 123: 11–20.

Edelman, G. M. 1992. *Bright Air, Brilliant Fire: On the Matter of the Mind.* New York: Basic.

Fadiman, D. 1988. *Why Do These Kids Love School?* Videotape. Menlo Park, Calif.: Concentric Media.

Gardner, H. 1985. *Frames of Mind: The Theory of Multiple Intelligences.* New York: Basic.

Gendlin, E. T. 1962. *Experiencing and the Creation of Meaning.* Glencoe, Calif.: The Free Press of Glencoe.

———. 1981. *Focusing.* 2d ed. New York: Bantam.

Goleman, D. 1995. *Emotional Intelligences: Why It Can Matter More than IQ.* New York: Bantam.

Gopnik, A., and A. N. Meltzoff. 1997. *Words, Thoughts, and Theories.* Cambridge, Mass.: MIT Press.

Halpern, D. 1989. *Thought and Knowledge: An Introduction to Critical Thinking.* Hillsdale, N.J.: Lawrence Erlbaum.

Hanh, T. N. 1976. *The Miracle of Mindfulness: A Manual on Meditation.* Boston: Beacon Press.

Hart, L. 1978. *Human Brain and Human Learning.* New York: Longman.

Helprin, M. 1975. "A Jew of Persia." In *A Dove of the East.* San Diego, Calif.: Harcourt, Brace, Jovanovich.

Jacobs, H. H., and L. Nadel. 1985. "Stress-Induced Recovery of Fears and Phobias." *Psychological Review* 92, 4: 512–31.

Jaworski, Joseph. 1996. *Synchronicity: The Inner Path of Leadership.* San Francisco: Berrett-Koehler.

Joyce, B., J. Wolf, and E. Calhoun. 1993. *The Self-Renewing School.* Alexandria, Va.: ASCD.

Kingsolver, B. 1990. *Animal Dreams.* New York: Harper Perennial.

Lakoff, G., and M. Johnson. 1980. *Metaphors We Live By.* Chicago: University of Chicago Press.

Langer, E. 1989. *Mindfulness.* Reading, Mass.: Addison-Wesley.

LeDoux, J. E. 1996. *The Emotional Brain.* New York: Simon and Schuster.

Lozanov, G. 1978. *Suggestology and Outlines of Suggestopedy.* New York: Gordon and Breach.

Maslow, A. H. 1968. *Towards a Psychology of Being.* New York: D. Van Nostrand.

O'Keefe, J., and L. Nadel. 1978. *The Hippocampus as a Cognitive Map.* Oxford: Clarendon Press.

Pert, C. B. 1997. *Molecules of Emotion.* New York: Scribner.

Peters, E. 1994. *A Morbid Taste for Bones.*

———. 1995. *Heretic's Apprentice.*

Restak, R. 1995. *Brainscapes.* New York: Hyperion.

Schacter, D. 1996. *Searching for Memory: The Brain, the Mind, and the Past.* New York: Basic.

Selye, H. 1978. *The Stress of Life.* Rev. ed. New York: McGraw-Hill.

Senge, P. M. 1990. *The Fifth Discipline: The Art and Practice of the Learning Organization.* New York: Doubleday Currency.

Vygotsky, L. S. 1978. *Mind in Society.* Cambridge, Mass.: Harvard University Press.

Wheatley, M. J. 1992. *Leadership and the New Science: Learning about Organization from an Orderly Universe.* San Francisco: Berrett-Koehler.

Whitehead, A. N. 1985. *The Aims of Education and Other Essays.* New York: Free Press.

Index

A

active learning, 16
active listening, 49
active processing, 216, 241, 246–47
active uncertainty, xiv, 157, 158–60, 201
adventurer, profile of, 211
advertisements, 142
age, learning and, 184
aha experience, 156, 161, 228–29
    activity, 229
amygdala, 26
Argyris, Chris
    and mental models, 7
art, 97, 135–36
    activity, 135–36
assessment, 235–36
    authentic, 216, 236
assumptions about education, 7–10, 18–20
attention, 33, 141–53, 175, 231
    activity, 143–46
    nature of, 144–46
    questions, 151–53
autobiographical memory, 132–33, 170–71, 175. *See also* locale memory
    activity, 133
    maps, 175
axons, 25

B

back-to-basics movement, 5
beliefs, 8–9, 189–90, 232. *See also* mental models
body language, 33
brain
    and attention, 32–33, 141–53
    and conscious learning, 34–35, 155–68
    designed for learning, 8, 27–28
    development of, 36–37, 183, 184
    and emotions, 30–31, 231. *See also* emotion
    hemispheres of, 32, 128
    and infants, 28
    and language, 28
    left, right, 32
    as living system, 26–27, 63–76
        activities, 66–68
        questions, 73–76
    and meaning, 28–30
    and memory, 35–36
    and music, effect on, 27, 128
    organization of, 38–39, 31
    and parts and wholes, 31–32, 127–39
    plasticity of, 25–26, 27, 184
    relaxation, effect on, 27
    research. *See* neurosciences
    resiliency of, 27
    social, 27–28, 42, 79–89, 215
        questions to explore, 87–89
    and spatial ability, 27, 95, 128
    split, 32, 135
    and stress, 27. *See also* stress
    and survival, 27–29. *See also* survival
    unique nature of, 38, 39, 209–17
        activities, 212–15
        questions, 215–17
brain-compatible learning, xi, 8, 19, 98, 247–51. *See also names of brain-compatible learning principles*
brain/mind, 26–39. *See also* brain, brain-compatible learning
    and body, 27, 64, 73, 170
    and input, 32
    and language development, 28–29
    and learning, 25–39, 187, 231
    principles, 26–39, 79–237, 257–58
    and values, 28
brainstorming, 14

C

Capra, Fritjof, 104
category traps, 122
celebrations, in learning community, 96
challenge, 9, 196, 233, 242
   activities, 197–204
   questions, 204–7
change
   educational, 6–7, 9, 13, 22–33, 256
   inhibitors, 71
   organizational, 23
   process groups and, 71
   systemic, 9, 10
child
   development of, 65, 67, 79, 93–94,
      156, 185, 190
   as living system, 66
coaching, peer, 259
cognition, 110, 156, 231
cognitive sciences, 231. *See also* neurosciences
community, 80–81, 81–83, 242–43, 253
concepts, teaching, 107–8, 223–26
concepts of education, central, 14, 46
conceptual learning, 225–27
connectedness, principles of, 46–47
connections, 12, 30–31, 46–47, 96, 132,
conscious processing, 155–68
   activities, 157–62
   problem solving and, 160–62,
   questions, 162–68
cooperative learning, 257
corpus callosum, 32
correct outcomes, 202
creative insight, 68, 156, 160–62, 196–97
Csikszentmihalyi, M., 195–96, 199
cultures, 95–96, 132, 210, 214
curriculum, 104, 107
   as patterns, 224–26, 246

D

deadlines, 202
deep meaning, 116, 156, 227, 231–33
   activity, 232–33
dendrites, 25, 183

director, profile of, 211
discipline, 236–37
distress, 196
downshifting, 37–38, 197, 200–201, 203–
   4
   questions, 204–7

E

education
   arts in, 97
   assumptions about, 7–10, 14–15
   and brain/mind principles, 26, 71
   central concepts of, 14
   challenges of, 3, 6, 80
   changes in, 6, 8–9, 22–23
   early childhood, 25, 235
   industrialized, ix, 10, 18–19, 72–73,
      80, 219, 222, 229, 235
   issues in, 4, 241
      checklist, 4
   problems in, 3
   questions to explore, 20–22
   undercurrents in, 5–6
embedding process, 179
emotion, 1, 30–31, 115–25, 156, 229, 231
   learning and, 30–31, 116–17, 229
   activities, 117–22
   questions, 123–25
   timeouts and, 157
eustress, 196
evaluator, profile of, 211–12
experiential learning, 10, 92, 98, 110,
      128, 136, 158, 168, 201–2, 239

F

fatigue, 37–38, 197
fear, 37–38
felt meaning, 116, 156, 227, 228–31
   activities, 228–29

G

groups. *See* process groups
guided experience, 219, 223, 234–37

H

Halpern, Diane, 142
Hart, Leslie, 197
hippocampus, 26
history, 176
hobbies, 177, 247
human
	development, 184–90
		activities, 185–90
		questions, 190–93
	growth in, 64–65

I

immersion. *See* orchestrated immersion
individuality, 47, 55, 56. *See also* brain, unique nature of
industrialization, education and, ix, 10, 18–19, 72–73, 80, 219, 222, 229, 235
inert knowledge, 222
infants, 33, 190
	and ability to hypothesize, 29
	and language development, 28
	and learning, 36–37, 93
	and numbers, 30
intrinsic motivation, 91–92, 116, 169, 196, 197–98, 231, 243–44
	checklist, 243–44

J

Johnson, M., 121
journals, xiii, 214
	using *MindShifts* as, 214
joy, 196

K

Kelly, George, 232
knowledge
	dynamical, xiv, 96, 151, 225, 227–30, 234
	inert, 222
	natural, 116
	real, 233. *See also* learning, genuine
	scholastic, 223–27
	surface, 222–23

activity, 223
technical, 223–27

L

Lakoff, G., 121
Langer, Ellen, 122, 246
language, 104, 121, 184
leadership, 44–45, 260
learning. *See also separate entries for subheads*
	active, 16
	and the brain, 25–39
	brain-compatible *See* brain-compatible learning *and individual principles*
	as central concept, 14
	and challenge, 37–38
	communities, xi, 9, 42, 85–86, 242–43, checklist for, 242–43
	complex, 9, 34, 92, 195–207
	conscious, 34–35
	developmental, ix, 36–37, 183–93
	and emotion, 30–31, 36, 37–38, 115–25, 185
	experiential, 92, 98, 110, 128, 136, 158, 168, 201–2, 239
	genuine, xiv, 92, 98, 162, 172, 201–3, 227
	guided experience vs. rote, 10, 92, 229
	joyful, 196, 212
	lifelong, 21, 27–28, 37
	meaningful, 19, 92, 123, 156, 178, 227
	and mental models, 13, 122
	outmoded assumptions about, 10, 14–15, 72–73, 80, 116–17
	and parts and wholes, 31, 64, 127–39, 231, 246
	and patterns, 25–39, 103–13, 115–25
	questions, 20
	schoolwide, 9
	styles, 8, 39
	and threat, 37–38, 80, 85
	unconscious, 34–35
learning community, 80–81, 81–83
	activities, 83–86
learning environment, 107, 111
LeDoux, Joseph, 34, 37

L (continued)

locale memory, 35–36, 132, 246
  activities, 174–75, 176–78
  maps, 177, 246
  questions, 179–81
Loewi, Otto, 155–56
Lozanov, G., 150

M

mapping, memory, 175
Maslow, Abraham, 231
mathematics, 17, 85
meaning, 28–29
  deep, 116, 156, 227, 231–33
    activity, 232–33
  felt, 116, 156, 227, 228–31
    activities, 228–29
  personal, 116, 202
  search for, 28–30, 91–113, 196
    activities, 93–98
    questions, 99–101
meaningful learning, xiii, 10, 156, 253–54
memorization, 10, 98, 116, 168, 169, 173–74, 176, 202, 234–35
memory, 26, 35–36, 167–81
  autobiographical, 132
  and emotion, 118, 168
  and environment, 33
  locale, 35, 132, 168, 170
  organization of, 35–36
  rote, 169
  spatial, 95, 170
  static vs. dynamic, 35–36
  subliminal, 33
  taxon, 35, 168–169
  taxon vs. locale, 35–36
  types of, 35–36
mental models
  changing, 17, 219, 253
  definition of, xiv, 7
  vs. espoused theories, 7, 16–17
  hidden, 17–18
  and learning, 13
  list of, 18–19
  and math, 17

  and problem solving, 13
  and professional development, 13–23, 253
  and research, 8
  role of, 13–23
  and teaching styles, 15–16
  as unconscious process, 34–35
metaphor, 109–10, 120–21
mind. *See* brain/mind
mindfulness, 157–58
motivation, 232
  extrinsic, 202
  intrinsic, 91–92, 116, 169, 196, 197–98, 231, 243–44
  Maslow's theory of, 92

N

Nadel, Lynn, 35, 168
neurons, 25, 36
neurosciences, 9, 19, 25–26, 28, 29
nurturer, profile of, 212

O

O'Keefe, J., 35, 168
opinions, personal, 47, 121–22
orchestrated immersion, 98, 216, 241, 244–45
  activities, 245, 248–49
orderliness, 242
outcomes
  correct, 202
  open-ended, 202, 203

P

parts and wholes, 31, 64, 127–39, 231, 246
  activities, 129–36
  questions, 111–13, 123–25
patterning, 29–31
  activities, 105–9, 117–22
  concepts and, 108–9
  curriculum and, 104, 107
  metaphors and, 109–10
  questions, 111–13, 123–25
patterns, 14, 210, 246

discovering, 31
and search for meaning, 103–13
perceptual styles, 210, 211–12
peripheral perception, 32–33, 141–53, 231
   activities, 146–50
   questions, 151–53
personal development, 256
personality, indicators of, 57, 210, 221–24
Peters, Ellis, 176
phonics, 5
physiology, learning and, 215
principles, brain/mind. *See* brain/mind, principles
problem solving, 13–14, 156, 160–62, 173
   study of, 48–49
process groups, xiv, 41–51, 256
   beginning, 54
   creating, xiv–xv, 43
   decisions about, 41–51, 55
   ending, 55, 260–61
   facilitator, 44–45
   guidelines, 46, 47, 53–59
   leadership of, 44–45, 260
   location of, 44
   objectives of, 41, 42, 43–44, 46, 49, 56
   ordered sharing in, 45, 46–48, 50, 158–60, 256
   participants in, 42–43, 53, 55
   preliminary gatherings, 50, 54
   routines, 260
   schedule of, 44, 55–56
   size of, 43, 50
   timekeeper, 48
processing
   active, 162
   conscious, 155–68
   unconscious, 155–68
professional development, 13, 253–61
projects, nature of, xiii, 134–35
proximal development, 188–89

R

relationships, social, 80–89
relaxed alertness, 217, 241, 242–44
   questions, 247–48

respect, 81–82
restrictive time lines, 202
rewards, 202
role models, 86, 189
rote learning. *See* memorization

S

safety, psychological, 53, 68–70, 148, 185, 201
school
   as community, 25
   environment, 142–43, 144, 148, 186, 201–2, 240–41
      activity, 135–36
science, teaching as, 95, 135–36
search for meaning, 91–113, 196
   activities, 93–98
   questions, 99–101
self, 64–65, 80, 94–95, 160, 197, 233
   protection of, 68, 71, 201
self-efficacy, 38, 199–200
   examination of, 157–58, 199–200
self-esteem, 70, 199
Selye, Hans, 196
Senge, Peter, 7, 13
senses, 143–44
sensory enhancement, 143–44, 231
skills, development of, 254–55
social brain, 27–28, 42, 79–89, 215
   questions to explore, 87–89
spatial memory, 95, 170
stories, 132–33
storytelling, 132–33, 134
stress, 196. *See also specific types*
students, role of, 16
surface knowledge, 222–23
survival, 86, 95, 148. *See also* safety, psychological
system
   adaptation of, 27, 71–72
   brain as, 26–27
   definition of, 26
   living, 27, 63–76
   social, 27–28
      activities, 66–72
   and survival, 27, 71

T

taxon memory, 35–36
    activities, 171–73, 176–78
    questions, 179–81
teaching, 14–16
    for expansion of natural knowledge, 231
    for meaning, 122, 241
    traditional, 122
teaching techniques, xiii, 87, 158, 241–42
    and technology, 254
technology, 80, 85, 254
television, 80
tests, 169, 173, 216, 235
theories, espoused, 7, 16–17
threat, 9, 196, 200–201, 242, 246
    activities, 201–4
    questions, 204–7

time lines, restrictive, 202

U

unconscious processing, 34–35, 153–62
    activities, 153–62
    questions, 163–65
undercurrents in education, 5–6

V

visual perception, 142, 184, 228
visual stimuli, 142, 143
Vygotsky, Lev, 188

W

Whitehead, Alfred North, 222
whole language, 5
workplace, 240–41

About the Authors

Geoffrey Caine, LL.M., an education and learning consultant, is an adjunct member of the faculty at the Whitehead Center for Lifelong Learning, the University of Redlands. He is co-author of *Making Connections: Teaching and the Human Brain, Education on the Edge of Possibility, Unleashing the Power of Perceptual Change,* and *The Re-Enchantment of Learning,* as well as several articles.

Renate Nummela Caine, Ph.D., is professor of education at California State University, San Bernardino, where she is also the executive director of the Center for Research in Integrative Learning and Teaching. Renate is co-author of *Making Connections: Teaching and the Human Brain, Education on the Edge of Possibility, Unleashing the Power of Perceptual Change,* and *The Re-Enchantment of Learning,* as well as several articles.

Sam Crowell, Ed.D., is associate professor of education at California State University, San Bernardino, where he is also a director of the Center for Research in Integrative Learning and Teaching. He has been an elementary teacher, a principal, and an administrator. Sam is the co-author of *The Re-Enchantment of Learning* and of several articles.

THE RE-ENCHANTMENT OF LEARNING
A Manual for Teacher Renewal and Classroom Transformation

by Sam Crowell, Ed.D.,
Renate Nummela Caine, Ph.D.,
and Geoffrey Caine, LL.M.
Professional Development

Boost your effectiveness in meeting today's challenges with strategies based on the new sciences. These field-tested methods have led to higher test scores.

You'll find—

- Brain-based teaching explained
- Processes to develop high-level teaching skills
- Innovative ways to tap creativity

1082-W . . . $32

MINDSHIFTS POSTERS
Principles of Connectedness

by Geoffrey Caine, LL.M., and Renate Nummela Caine, Ph.D.
photographs by Debbie Crowell
Grades K–12+

You'll have a new way to support your growth in Mindshifts process groups with these inspiring posters! Let your imagination soar with elegant posters that feature the Principles of Connectedness from the best-selling *MindShifts* book. Each process group begins with an ordered sharing based on one of these principles.

You'll discover many ways to use the posters and add color and inspiration to your classroom. Use the posters—

- For discussion in Mindshifts process group sessions and ordered sharing
- As prompts for student essays and exploring curriculum
- As a set of general reminders about the purpose of the group process
- As a complete package for exploration of school change along with the *MindShifts* book and video

12 full-color, 11" X 17", posters and one 8 1/2" X 11" sheet of Suggestions for Use.
1821-W . . . $29

Call, Write, or FAX for your FREE Catalog!

Qty.	Item #	Title	Unit Price	Total
	1707-W	Windows to the Mind, Vol. 3	$149	
	1708-W	Windows to the Mind, Vol. 4	$149	
	1712-W	Windows to the Mind, Vols. 3 & 4	$248	
	1082-W	The Re-Enchantment of Learning	$32	
	1821-W	MindShifts Posters	$29	

Name _____

Address _____

City _____

State _____ Zip _____

Phone (____) _____

E-mail _____

Method of payment (check one):

❑ Check or Money Order ❑ Visa

❑ MasterCard ❑ Purchase Order Attached

Credit Card No. _____

Expires _____

Signature _____

Subtotal	
Sales Tax (AZ residents, 5%)	
S & H (10% of subtotal, min. $4.00)	
Total (U.S.funds only)	

CANADA: add 22% for S & H and G.S.T.

☎ ORDER TODAY!

Please include your phone number in case we have questions about your order.

To order write or call:

Zephyr Press ®

REACHING THEIR HIGHEST POTENTIAL

P.O. Box 66006-W
Tucson, AZ 85728-6006

1-800-232-2187
520-322-5090
FAX 520-323-9402
http://www.zephyrpress.com

Make a Smooth Transition to Educational Change with These Powerful Tools from Caine, Caine, and Crowell!

Windows to the Mind, Vol. 3
TEACHING AND THE HUMAN BRAIN

by Geoffrey Caine, L.L.M., and Renate Nummela Caine, Ph.D.
Staff Development

Here's an information-packed introduction to important new theories in teaching and learning that are changing education today. You'll see a practical new vision of how education can adapt to the challenge of preparing students for tomorrow's world. The Caines also present vital new information on—

- Educational outcomes based on meaningful learning
- Teaching for dynamical knowledge
- Downshifting and self-efficacy
- The complexity of change

Teaching and the Human Brain is great for your own education and for use in workshops and study groups. Look to the 20-page discussion guide for additional support on the presentation and suggestions on how to use it effectively.

60-minute, full-color, VHS video. 20-page discussion guide.
1707-W . . . $149

Windows to the Mind, Vol. 4
MINDSHIFTS

by Geoffrey Caine, LL.M., Renate Nummela Caine, Ph.D., and Sam Crowell, Ed.D.
Staff Development

Here's the how-to video you need to help bring meaningful change to your school. Watch this video to see mindshifts process groups in action and discover the need for educators to transform their thinking collectively.

MindShifts video will guide you through the mindshifts process to help you transform your beliefs and theories into mental models. You'll find help on—

- Exploring the problems of system change
- Understanding different instructional approaches
- Discovering why collective change is most effective
- Seeing how a group functions and anticipating key issues
- Transforming those ideas into mental models that really work

60-minute, full-color, VHS video. 20-page discussion guide.
1708-W . . . $149

SPECIAL OFFER

SAVE $50!
Order both videos and SAVE $50!
1712-W . . . $248